MESSENGERS OF

THE RISEN SON IN

THE LAND OF THE

RISING SUN

MESSENGERS OF THE RISEN SON IN THE LAND OF THE RISING SUN

SINGLE WOMEN MISSIONARIES IN JAPAN

BONNIE MILLER

LEAFWOOD
PUBLISHERS

Abilene, Texas

Messengers of the Risen Son in the Land of the Rising Sun

Copyright 2008 by Bonnie Miller

ISBN 978-0-89112-567-9

Printed in the United States of America

Cover design by Rick Gibson

For information contact:
Leafwood Publishers, Abilene, Texas
1-877-816-4455 toll free
www.leafwoodpublishers.com

08 09 10 11 12 / 7 6 5 4 3 2 1

Cover photos: (l-r) Alice Miller, Sarah Andrews, Loduska Wirick, Lillie Cypert.

Dedication

With great admiration for the work they did, the sacrifices they made, the difficulties they endured, and the inspiration of their lives, this book is dedicated to the single women who have gone throughout the world to take the gospel to the lost. May their number increase.

CONTENTS

LIST OF PHOTOGRAPHS

ACKNOWLEDGMENTS

Surely, no book is ever written single-handedly. This one certainly wasn't. It is largely the result of the encouragement and initiative of Jerry Rushford, my friend and mentor at Pepperdine University. He was the one who first suggested that I should write a book about Sarah Andrews. He then contacted Sarah's family, and after persuading them that I should be the one to write a book about Sarah, he called Leonard Allen and convinced him that he should publish it. Jerry continued to facilitate the project by providing resources (including books from his library), introductions to other knowledgeable people, and suggestions for improvement after reading the first draft. Lessons learned while working on other projects with Jerry have guided me through this publication process. He is a treasured and irreplaceable friend.

Sarah's nephew Dan Andrews and niece Bettie Lundy supplied much of the initial information about the Andrews family and Sarah's life. Dan flew me to Nashville to meet with the family and do research in Lipscomb University's Beaman Library, the Disciples of Christ Historical Society, and Sarah's hometown of Dickson, Tennessee. While enjoying the hospitality of Randy and Rhonda Lowry in Nashville (who even loaned me their car to drive), I was able to spend a marvelous week of uninterrupted research. Aided by Mac Ice at the Disciples of Christ Historical Society, I reveled in reading primary source materials and seeing in photos the faces of the women I was writing about.

Shawn Daggett, at Harding University Graduate School of Religion, was in the process of completing his dissertation on the subject of mission work among the Restoration Movement. He graciously shared his scanned images of the early missionary journals that provided the bulk of information about the early workers in Japan.

Brenda Nixon completed a biography of her great-aunt Lillie Cypert in 2006 and shared the compiled information and photos. She had gleaned much information from one of Lillie's "children," Steve Yanai, who provided the pictures of Lillie.

Harry Robert Fox Jr. preserved letters he exchanged with Sarah Andrews over the years and those became a rich source of information about the post-war years.

Ministers in Japan such as Motoyuki Nomura, Yukikazu Obata and Sami Sagitani have been my eyes and spell-checkers. Having never been to Japan myself, they verified information and names of towns that clarified where churches were located. My daughter, Chelan Metcalf, also served as a proofreader and made suggestions to improve the readability of the manuscript.

Others have helped along the way to send a photo, provide a date, suggest another source, or share information. Those included Craig Churchill and Doug Foster at Abilene Christian University's Center for Restoration Studies, Chris Flanders of ACU's Halbert Institute for Missions, Michael Clark at Cascade College's E. W. McMillan Library, Michio Nagai, Tom Olbright, Mary Jane Calhoun at Johnson Bible College, and Mike Casey before his death.

Photos were provided by some of the women's family members as well as total strangers. Warrick Barrett, whom I met on the Internet, put me in touch with Akira Komatsu who arranged for the use of a photo of Loduska Wirick's tombstone taken by Shigeyuki Matsuoka. Tomoko Iizuka, another of Komatsu's contacts, provided additional photos of the Wirick tombstone. Nancy Prosser, a descendant of Rose Johnson Calderwood, filled in missing information about her grandmother.

The library at Northwest Christian College in Eugene, Oregon, houses sets of *World Call* and *Christian Standard*. These were invaluable for learning about the Christian Church and Disciples of Christ's missionaries.

I have been blessed for over twenty-four years to minister on staff with the Vancouver Church of Christ in Washington State. Such an encouraging atmosphere in which to work, co-workers to labor and consult with, and supportive elders that have allowed me a very flexible schedule in order to research and write have contributed to the completion of this project. We serve a great God.

Bonnie Miller
February 2008

PREFACE

As the international date line in the Pacific Ocean marks the beginning of each new day, Japan is the first country, excluding Australia and Siberia, on which the sun shines. For this reason it became known as the Land of the Rising Sun. It consists of a string of islands stretching a distance similar to that from Maine to Florida and enjoys the same variation in climate as the eastern United States—snow in the northern regions and hot, humid weather in the southern areas. The total area of Japan is roughly 147,000 square miles, less than that of California.

As the nineteenth century came to a close, Japan was a mysterious group of islands that had been closed to the Western world until 1853 when Commodore Matthew Calbraith Perry sailed into Yokohama Harbor and demanded that Japan open trade with the Western world. For 250 years Japan had virtually no contact with anyone outside her borders and it had been a capital crime for a Japanese to confess faith in Christ.

The religion of Japan at the beginning of the twentieth century was a mixture of Shinto and Buddhism. Shintoism involves hundreds of shrines where adherents leave offerings to the idols and worship countless gods, including devotees' ancestors. Until the end of World War II, the emperor was believed to be directly descended from a god and was therefore divine and worshipped as such. Buddhism is more about a philosophy of life.

Government edicts were issued as late as 1868 prohibiting Christianity. "The evil sect Christian is strictly forbidden; suspected persons should be reported and rewards will be given," the ban stated. Another edict, translated by one of the early missionaries, was even stronger: "So long as the sun shall warm the earth, let no Christian be so bold as to come to Japan; and let all know that the king of Spain himself, or the Christian's god, or the great God of all, if he violate this command, shall pay for it with his head."

The Western religion had been blamed for the introduction of opium usage in China, and Japan feared the same impact on their nation if Christian missionaries were unrestrained. The laws forbade a missionary to ask a native to accept Christianity, and the penalty for any native to profess the Christian faith was death. These edicts were not removed until 1873. Even then, no foreigner could live outside the treaty ports. Passports could be obtained, but they were good for only six months. Foreigners could be employed by a school or individual to teach English outside the treaty cities, or they could request permission to live elsewhere if they were engaged in scientific research or sought recovery of their health. Consequently, when Protestant missionaries arrived before the edicts were lifted, most lived and worked within the city of Tokyo or were employed as English language teachers.

During the years when preaching the gospel was illegal, the Protestant and Jesuit missionaries made good use of their time. They studied the language, translated the Scriptures into Japanese, and prepared grammars and dictionaries that would be useful to other missionaries in later years. Their compassion extended to the destitute, which made a favorable impression on their host country. In 1899 when the restrictions were finally lifted, there were 625 Protestant missionaries in Japan and, of the forty million or more residents, only 39,240 claimed some form of Christianity.

Slowly Japan began to accept that Christianity was not a threat to their national well-being. Rather, they correlated the advances of Western civilization with the Christian religion of the Western world. The character of those bringing this "new religion" to Japan also determined its acceptance. The missionaries' compassion and demonstration of God's love for all people communicated more fluently than their mastery of the complex Japanese language.

INTRODUCTION

The Restoration Movement was more than twenty years behind other Protestant efforts to evangelize Japan. The first missionaries to the Land of the Rising Sun sent by the American Restoration Movement sailed on September 27, 1883. Since they were sent by the Foreign Christian Missionary Society, many who now claim membership in the a cappella Churches of Christ or the Christian Churches/Churches of Christ are unfamiliar with their names. The Disciples of Christ, a third group descended from the American Restoration Movement, have maintained a closer bond with the missionary societies.

Missionary societies had been a point of contention among Restoration churches since their inception prior to the Civil War. The American Christian Missionary Society (1849), the Christian Woman's Board of Missions (1874), the Foreign Christian Missionary Society (1875) and later the United Christian Missionary Society (1920) were all parachurch organizations of the Restoration Movement. Although the division was not officially recognized until 1906, by the 1880s there were clear differences between those who would be known primarily as Churches of Christ and those who would take the name Christian Churches and later Disciples of Christ.

The story of the Restoration Movement in Japan is bound up in all three streams of the American movement, however, and no story of Restoration missionaries in Japan would be complete without representatives from all three streams. Furthermore, these early messengers found common ground whenever possible and tried to avoid differences of opinion that threatened to divide the Movement in the U.S. toward the end of the nineteenth century.

Sadly, these differences that eventually split the brotherhood in the States would also result in a chasm among those working in foreign fields. Naturally, the controversy over missionary societies had the most pronounced effect on those in the field. The "antis," mostly a cappella churches, were those opposed to missionary societies, claiming the church as the only missionary society authorized in Scripture. Most of the Christian Churches (Disciples of Christ) endorsed the societies as an efficient means to achieve a scriptural mandate to evangelize the world.

The basic problem lay in how to apply the "silence of Scripture." If the Bible didn't specifically address an issue, did that mean it was permitted or unauthorized and thereby prohibited? Missionary societies fell into this gray area of silence.

Coupled with a similar question over the use of instrumental music in worship, churches began to go their separate ways and two distinct fellowships developed. A third group formed following the formation of the United Christian Missionary Society in 1920 bringing the Disciples of Christ into existence as a separate body.

Through the early years of the twentieth century, however, all three groups preached the same gospel calling for the immersion of repentant sinners to receive the forgiveness of sins. Thus their work in Japan, although carried out by different methods, brought about the same results—sinners turning from idol worship to embrace the God of the Bible and uniting with Christ as their Savior.

The *Christian Standard*, a publication edited by Isaac Errett in Cleveland and then Cincinnati, expressed the ideal of some when it reported, "our devotion to the 'church method' and the society method does not hinder us rejoicing in the independent method. . . . With us the work is everything, the method merely incidental and subject to constant revision."

The complete story of the church in Japan is broad and encompasses married couples, single men and women, and native evangelists. This book endeavors to tell the story of a small segment of those who went to Japan before World War II—the single women who dared to do what few men were willing to do. They left their families and friends to cross nearly six thousand miles of ocean, alone, in order to take the gospel to the people of Japan in the early years of the twentieth century.

CHAPTER ONE

THE FIRST FOREIGNERS

Sent by the Foreign Christian Missionary Society, Charles E. Garst and George T. Smith, along with their wives, Laura Garst and Josephine Smith, and the Smith's six-year-old daughter, Elsie, left San Francisco on Thursday, September 27, 1883. They arrived in Yokohama harbor on October 18 after three weeks on the ocean. The snow-capped peak of Mount Fuji, a dormant volcano considered sacred by many Japanese, rose above the narrow streets of Tokyo to welcome them. They spent the first month in a hotel there and then rented a house in Akita on the northwest coast since foreigners were not allowed to own property in Japan until 1910. It could be argued that little Elsie was the first "single woman" from the Christian Church to go to Japan. Unfortunately, her tour of duty in Japan was brief (less than two years) as her mother, in the advanced stages of Bright's disease when she arrived in Japan, died following the birth of the Smiths' second child on March 23, 1885. The baby also died within a month. About three months later friends sent Elsie back to the States to the care of relatives.

Not long after settling in at Akita, a fire swept through the city destroying nearly the entire town. The Smith–Garst residence was spared when the wind shifted, a turn of events the missionaries attributed to the hand of God. Seeing the opportunity to put their faith into action, they opened their school building to house the displaced and feed those affected. This helped break down the resistance of the Japanese people as they saw the foreigners were genuinely concerned for their well-being. All religious meetings had to be suspended for a time a few months later when a cholera epidemic blanketed the city taking over 200,000 lives.

Although these first Restoration missionaries in Japan were sent by the Society, many of the independent missionaries who came later were acquainted with them and benefited from the foundation of trust and good will they established. J. M. McCaleb, a member of the first group of independent missionaries, found it essential to maintain a friendly attitude and show respect for others who held variant opinions. "Differences of importance should be recognized and acted upon," he said, "but where people agree they should realize it and use these points of agreement as a foundation on which to build till agreement is reached on all points of importance."

McCaleb's statement explains why some missionaries did not consider their attachment to the Society essential to spread the gospel. Some workers came to Japan under the direction of the Society but later broke off their connection and became independent. Others began as independent missionaries but later joined the Society. A few were loosely connected to the Society, drawing partial support from various local groups as well as from individuals and churches. And some independent missionaries respected the Society although they remained unconnected to it.

Before World War I, most Protestant missionaries were men. The balance shifted thereafter as women maintained two-thirds of Protestant mission work and missions became the preeminent cause for women in most denominations. Since some foreign cultures considered it improper for men to engage women in conversation, it became necessary to recruit women to assist in the evangelization of native women. This was true of Old Japan where the women were dominated by the men to such an extent that wives were expected to commit suicide following their husband's death. Beginning about 1860, a few single women began to respond to the appeal for workers to go abroad. Most female missionaries went as teachers and focused on reaching women and children although their English Bible classes usually included men as well.

The year 1892 marked the arrival of the first totally independent missionaries from the Restoration Movement in Japan. W. K. Azbill had been a missionary in Jamaica for ten years under the oversight of the Christian Woman's Board of Missions.

As the controversy over the Society brewed, Azbill set about to prove that evangelization could be carried out independently with direct support from churches and individuals. He assumed that churches opposed to the Society would be willing to contribute directly to foreign missionaries. In reality, only a few gave modestly while most provided nothing.

Azbill's endeavor was watched closely as a test case to see if missionary work without institutional support could succeed. One Restoration paper at the time, the *Christian Evangelist,* predicted: "Its failure will demonstrate either that the volunteer plan is not the Bible plan, or that the churches and individuals opposed to missionary societies and contending for the Bible plan are not as much in earnest in missionary matters as they claim to be." The *Evangelist* proved correct. Although willing men and women were recruited to the mission field, they found themselves depending on the providence of God for their sustenance as contributions from churches and individuals were meager and irregular, thus demonstrating the lack of commitment to foreign missions.

When Azbill began his project, the name of J. M. McCaleb was recommended to him as someone who might be willing to accompany him to Japan. McCaleb was a newlywed when Azbill approached him. After conferring and praying with his bride Della, they determined that this was God's call. The McCalebs were crucial to the success of this mission effort as Azbill was going to Japan without his wife and the only other missionaries he had been able to recruit were two single women. He later confessed to McCaleb that he would not have been able to go without the McCalebs due to the impropriety of a lone man escorting two single women.

A young Japanese man, Kakujiro Ishikawa, who had been converted by Azbill and McCaleb in San Francisco just prior to their sailing, also accompanied the group. Once back in his homeland, Ishikawa set about converting his father and mother and four others. Later Ishikawa became president of the Christian Church mission school near Tokyo.

Before the end of 1915, McCaleb reported 721 converts and the establishment of eight churches in the twenty-three years he had been in the country. However, he sadly added that about half of those converts had either died, fallen away, or their whereabouts were no longer known.

CHAPTER TWO

THE FIRST SINGLE WOMEN

Azbill's two female recruits, Lucia Scott and Carme Hostetter, were the first independent single female missionaries in Japan. Both Lucia and Carme had been students at the Disciples of Christ school, Hiram College, and belonged to the Student Volunteer Movement, a mission group at Hiram. Azbill made it clear that they would not be receiving funds from any missionary society but would depend on support from churches alone and simply "trust in the Lord."

Prior to departing for Japan, Azbill gathered his little group of independent missionaries in Indianapolis where they boarded a train to San Francisco. The night before their departure from Indianapolis, the Governor of Indiana was invited to speak and toast them at a gala reception held in their honor. Due to a mix-up in scheduling, the governor was unable to attend but a large crowd of fellow believers sent them off with well-wishes and prayer. The little volunteer group departed with high hopes as they traveled through Kansas, Colorado and Southern California, visiting churches along the way to solicit funds and draw attention to their endeavor.

The group sailed from San Francisco March 26, 1892, and arrived in the port of Yokohama on April 12. Because the governmental restrictions concerning where foreigners could live were still in effect, they set up their base of operations within Tokyo in the Kanda and Yotsuya areas. They found the Yotsuya Ward was an urban slum populated with lepers and those with other diseases, the blind and the lame, and children without adequate clothing or food. When ward inhabitants rose in the mornings, they pawned their beds for enough yen to buy food for the day. If they earned or begged enough during the day to redeem the bed, they had it to sleep on another night. Lucia and Carme learned that children were sometimes kidnapped and sold to work in the factories, and they immediately set about establishing a charity school. The school became known as the Yotsuya Mission and in 1896 a six-room school building was erected.

Although located in a slum area, the Yotsuya property was in a very desirable location given its proximity to the Crown Prince's palace and the nobles' school where the children of the country's leaders were educated. When the Japanese government began to provide public education for all children several years later, the mission ceased operation of the charity school but continued to offer classes and eventually expanded to several other locations.

Lucia Scott, Carme Hostetter, W. K. Azbill, Della and J. M. McCaleb
Photo courtesy of Disciples of Christ Historical Society

In addition to running the school, Lucia assisted in Sunday services, taught English ten hours a week, gave children singing lessons, assisted in women's meetings, and studied the language. Her work with the school resulted in the organization of two churches. Lucia and Carme labored in Yotsuya together, teaching and visiting in the Japanese homes, until 1897 when Lucia was obliged to return to her homeland on account of the serious illness of her mother. She arrived in Seattle on August 3 on the *S.S. Olympia*. She never returned to Japan but lived with her brother on a ranch in Southern California until her death in 1926. (See the appendix for biographical data on each of these female missionaries.)

Carme Hostetter was born in Ohio in 1869 and educated at Ada Normal School (Normal Schools were training institutions for teachers). In Japan, she began the Kanda Ward school, which she later turned over to J. M. McCaleb. She rented a lot, "put up a good house," employed two teachers, and began two classes that grew to fifty children. The children received Japan's standard educational curriculum plus an hour of singing and Bible study daily. Some of the girls were also taught sewing. In addition to this day school, Carme conducted women's meetings, taught Sunday school, led a Bible class in her home for young men, and instructed English ten hours a week in a large Japanese school. Regardless of what day of the week a children's Bible school was conducted, the Japanese referred to it as a "Sunday school."

Her first furlough back to the States came after she had completed five years of work in Japan. She arrived in Seattle on June 25, 1897, aboard the *S.S. Tacoma* and continued from there to her home in Ohio. During this furlough, she enrolled at Nashville Bible School (now Lipscomb University). From there, she went to Hiram College in Ohio where she took business and liberal arts courses.

In 1900, Carme became discouraged about working as an independent missionary when she didn't get the encouragement she felt she should have. She joined the Foreign Christian Missionary Society and returned to Japan under their direction. She was stationed at Sendai, a city in the northern area of the mainland, where she conducted Sunday schools and classes for women and children. In the summer of 1904, she went to Karuizawa, a famous summer resort for foreigners about ninety miles from Tokyo. The little town was located at the foot of Mount Asama in a valley created by an ancient volcano. Due to its three thousand–foot altitude, it provided a cool respite from the city heat. There Carme met another American—Martin Mosser Smyser, an English instructor in Hagi in the western part of Japan.

Smyser's diaries indicate he was instantly attracted to this American missionary woman. Back in Sendai, Carme began to correspond with Smyser. On March 3, 1905, he sent her a letter of proposal, and they were married two months later on May 13. As a result of Carme's teaching, Smyser was baptized and together they moved to Osaka, the second largest city in Japan. Carme resigned from the Society and went to work for a commercial college while assisting the work of the Christian missionaries.

A daughter was born to the Smysers in 1906 after which they determined to return to the States for more formal education. After completing his studies at White's Bible School in New York City, Smyser was ordained to the ministry in January of 1910. For the next four years, they lived in Maine where he served as a home missionary among the lumbermen for the Congregationalists. In 1914, they returned to Japan and worked in the city of Yokote, a remote town in Akita Prefecture on the northwest coast of Honshu, Japan's main island. Modern conveniences were so limited in the isolated area that Carme had to go to Tokyo to have glasses made for her daughter and to have some dental work done in December 1916. She felt the work was worth the sacrifice when fourteen baptisms were reported in their city in 1917.

Marriage to this strong-willed German, who had not been raised in the church as Carme had, caused a strain on the relationship. In 1918, Carme took advantage of the opportunity for a temporary separation in order to bring their daughter, Lois, to California to attend school. Unable to afford a private school, Carme looked up her former co-worker Lucia Scott who was living in San Jose at the time, rented a room from her, and placed Lois in public school. After Lois graduated from the University of California at Berkeley, Carme took a position as matron of a retirement home for missionaries in Claremont.

In 1932, Smyser voyaged to the United States to meet his supporters and ask Carme to return with him to Yokote. Carme decided she could not endure the cold, damp weather, tremendous amount of housework, financial strain, and differing philosophies of how mission work should be conducted. In addition to these differences,

Smyser had introduced instrumental music into the churches he worked with, and in cases of extreme illness he used sprinkling for baptism. She bid him farewell for the last time in June 1932 and he returned to Japan alone where he died in Akita in 1955. Carme was laid to rest in Oak Park Cemetery in Claremont, California, following her death on July 16, 1945.

Alice Miller

Photo courtesy of Disciples of Christ Historical Society

CHAPTER THREE

ALICE MILLER:
A FAITHFUL, SELF-DENYING WORKER

When Lucia Scott returned to the U.S. in 1897, Alice Miller took her place. Azbill had returned to the States within a year of his arrival in Japan for the purpose of recruiting more workers. He visited Earlington, Kentucky, and found Alice in June 1894. She told him that she had long desired to be a missionary and would gladly go if she were sure she could "be of any use."

Alice's great-great-great nephew, historian Earl West, recalled that Alice's father had owned a store in Cadiz, Kentucky, that was burned down during the Civil War. He then moved his family to Evansville, Indiana, where Alice began teaching school. She relocated to Earlington, Kentucky, where she continued to teach and became the principal of the school. Knowing how well-equipped she was for educational work, Azbill convinced her that her skills could be put to good use in Japan.

She gave him permission to announce that she was willing to go as soon as her support could be secured. The announcement appeared in the *Christian Evangelist* that June, and within six months her support had been provided. She left for Japan in December, arriving February 2, 1895. A close friend of Alice, Mrs. McEwen, was so moved by her decision that she arranged for Alice to receive regular income from the rental of a house Mrs. McEwen owned. Mrs. McEwen even ensured that, in the event that Alice needed to return from the mission field due to poor health, the income would continue. "Should her friend suffer the loss of her health on the mission field," Azbill explained, "she would deserve this support after her return." Azbill noted that as she was "committing herself to the care of God, it is as strong an expression of faith in His providence as she is able to show."

During her first year in Japan, Alice experienced a serious disappointment. Her house and all its contents were destroyed in a fire. Through a mutual acquaintance—Kakujiro Ishikawa (the young Japanese man who had been converted in San Francisco prior to the departure of Azbill's first group)—Alice made friends with Shizuko Iwamoto, a Japanese writer known for translating "Little Lord Fauntleroy." The Iwamatos had also lost their home in a fire and lived with Ishikawa for a time afterward. It may have been this mutual tragedy that drew the two women together in a bond of friendship. Sadly, Mrs. Iwamoto died within the year. A few years later, Alice narrowly escaped another house fire when a nearby home went up in flames during the night. Only the asbestos roof on her house saved it from the sparks and burning embers that fell on it.

Immediately upon arriving in Japan, Alice immersed herself in the work. She continued Lucia Scott's work with the Yotsuya Mission and taught four English classes and three Bible classes each week. The English classes, which she taught in her home, developed into a fully organized work with Sunday school, preaching, prayer meeting, women's meeting, and Bible classes. For twelve years, Alice had from one to four young Japanese girls living with her as she trained them. Her influence crossed gender lines as at least six young men under her influence became gospel preachers. She also welcomed visitors from the U.S. who lived with her for extended periods of time. Her lengthy letters, published in the church paper *Tokyo Christian*, were filled with news of the meetings, the activities and health of individual Christians, and plans for enlarging the work as guided by the Spirit.

After four years in Japan, Alice spent some time in Hawaii for a much-needed rest in 1899. Her annual report for 1904 confirmed that she continued her busy routine upon her return. She reported having fifty-five children in the charity school, 225 in the Sunday school, and twelve to fifteen women in Bible study. In addition, she led relief work on behalf of the widows and orphans of Japanese soldiers' families. It was during this time that Japan and Russia had gone to war to determine dominance over Manchuria and Korea. Japan was victorious but suffered great loss of life. During this Russo-Japanese War, Alice sewed clothing for the destitute children of soldiers, providing most of the material herself. About this time, she moved into a new house that she shared with six Japanese women including four girls whom she was supporting. Dr. Gertrude Remington, another missionary, also lived with her for several months.

Her Christmas programs included treating all of the children in her school to candy, cake, fruit, and clothing and each of the thirty mothers were given a cake of soap.

In 1906, Alice resigned from her work to return to the States for health reasons. The change rejuvenated her, and she was able to resume her work in Japan, arriving on November 7, 1907. Her return surprised her co-workers who had thought her health so poor that she would not be coming back. But she refused to abandon the people she had grown to love, especially the children whom she was teaching.

Alice primarily served the poorest, most destitute children in Tokyo. Their living conditions were described as the most wretched slums where hopeless men, weary women, and dirty children crowded together in rickety hovels unfit for human habitation. Alice felt a desire to teach these children how to live decently and contribute to society. The *Tokyo Christian*, a paper published by co-worker W. D. Cunningham, urged readers to contribute to her work in order that she could "put life and hope and energy into this dark district."

CUNNINGHAM TAKES CHARGE OF YOTSUYA

In 1903, Alice invited William Dayton Cunningham, an independent missionary by default, to take charge of the Yotsuya Mission because there was no one to follow up on evangelistic contacts. Previously, around 1898, Cunningham had contracted polio and had been partially paralyzed on his left side. He twice applied to the Society to be sent to Japan, but both times they refused his request due to his health condition. When he determined that God and the Missionary Society were not one in the same, he decided to answer what he believed was God's call to go forth independently instead. He built a house and chapel in the Yotsuya compound and took over the work that Carme, Lucia, and Alice established.

Although located next to a Buddhist temple, the Yotsuya Mission was one of the most successful efforts undertaken by the independent missionaries. By 1905, twelve years since its inception, the mission was responsible for the baptisms of 185 people, including students, teachers, soldiers, civil officers, and businessmen. Most had been converted through the use of English Bible classes. The students in the school were taught the usual subjects plus Bible lessons, sewing, and "neatness in person and dress."

Even though Cunningham took charge of the Yotsuya Mission, Azbill insisted that the "first essential work in the founding of that Mission—the winning of the respect and confidence of the people on behalf of Christianity—was done by Miss Scott and Miss Miller during the first eleven years of its existence. They laid the foundation, and Mr. Cunningham builded thereupon."

The Yotsuya chapel was a beautiful facility with electric lights and fine furnishings. Alice donated the pulpit stand; Lavinia Oldham, another single missionary, provided the pulpit Bible; and Kate Johnson, also a single missionary, gave a clock. In 1905, following the end of the Russo-Japanese War, riots in Tokyo resulted in mob destruction of twelve church buildings. However, due to the relief work by the Yotsuya Mission among the families of Japanese soldiers, a squad of soldiers guarded the chapel twenty-four hours a day for a week. The chapel door was stoned twice and one door was broken in but no other damage was sustained.

When Cunningham and his wife Emily went on furlough in 1908, Alice resumed complete oversight of the Yotsuya Mission. "It is a pleasure to know that we leave the work in such excellent hands," Cunningham wrote. "We ask that friends will remember Miss Miller and her extra burdens in prayer." Cunningham continued, "As the years go by we appreciate more and more the privilege of working with Miss Alice Miller, than whom it would be difficult to find a more consecrated Christian woman, or a more efficient mission worker. Besides helping in all the other work, Miss Miller has special charge of two women's meetings, two Sunday schools, one day school for poor children, and the training of several Japanese girls. Her teachers and Bible women are trained and faithful workers."

Cunningham held Alice in such high regard that he even made arrangements that, in the event of his death, she would be part of a committee of five who would administer the Yotsuya property that was now in his name. This arrangement was altered to omit Alice in later years after a difference of opinion arose between them.

FROM YATSUYA TO SENDAGAYA

In the fall of 1908, Alice informed her supporters that the Yotsuya Mission school was going to have to be moved as a result of the anticipated Exhibition of 1912 that would be located on land adjoining the mission property. The government was too embarrassed to have the expected guests see the impoverished slum and decided to relocate the people to another part of the city. A street was to be constructed where the school building stood. Cunningham urged his supporters to aid Alice with funds to move the school. He praised her as "a worker of rare spirit and ability. She has been especially successful in training young men and young women for Christian work. Her women's meetings, charity school and Bible Schools are among the best."

As a result of this forced relocation, two new mission stations were begun. One was at Sendagaya and included an industrial school that Alice oversaw. Opened on May 15, 1910, this had been Alice's dream for several years. She envisioned an institution where poor children could receive a proper education, Bible instruction, and learn a trade by which they could support themselves honorably. Upon completion, it featured one room on the first floor for the school with another large room for industrial work. A bathroom, dining room, and kitchen were at the rear. Upstairs there were four comfortable rooms for the teachers' quarters.

Prior to Cunningham's arrival at Yotsuya, no instrumental music had been used in the church services there, but he introduced it against the wishes of those who had founded the Mission. Alice neither favored nor opposed the use of instrumental music in worship but did ask for and received a small organ to be used in the music classes she taught. An appeal was made in the April 1909 *Tokyo Christian* requesting "a medium sized cabinet organ which is not in use."

Two months later it was reported that Mrs. W. E. Compton of Cleveland had donated one of two organs Alice needed in her schools. There is no mention of when the second organ was obtained. It is known that the Yotsuya Mission had an Estey organ in 1910 and is likely the one Compton gave. Many years later, Motoyuki Nomura, a native Restoration preacher in Japan, was able to locate and acquire a Mason-Hamlin organ that belonged to Alice.

J. M. McCaleb felt compelled to inform his supporters that the Yotsuya Mission had begun using instrumental music in its worship services. He regretted having to report this change but, because he frequently mentioned and commended this mission work, he felt he must let the church back home know given his well-known opposition to the use of the instruments in worship. "They have a right to expect that any work I would commend would be free from this evil," he said. He tried to persuade Cunningham against using it, but he reported that Cunningham felt it should not be made a test of fellowship and therefore placed the blame for any division over its use at the feet of the anti-instrumental people.

Alice felt McCaleb was "trying to control the details of her work," according to McCaleb. However, in deference to him, she did not use the instrument whenever McCaleb was present. Alice and Cunningham could not agree on the matter, however, and while she was in the States on furlough in 1913, he bought the lot on which her home in the Yotsuya Mission compound was built and demanded that she remove her house. In her absence and at her request, McCaleb sold the house for her. B. F. Coulter, a Christian merchant and preacher in California who was also from Kentucky, had originally contributed the funds for the purchase of the house for Alice.

During this 1913 furlough, Alice's sisters in Kentucky urged her to stay in the States but she declined and, at the age of sixty, went back to Japan in the fall of 1914. With her house at the Yotsuya Mission sold, she purchased a Japanese house in Sendagaya where she had previously begun the industrial school. She remodeled the house to accommodate church meetings downstairs with her living quarters upstairs. One of two Bible women she employed, Masai Kurachi, kept up the work among the women and children at Sendagaya while Alice had been gone. About twenty women attended the services, and some of the older girls began, in turn, to evangelize their mothers. Even some of the neighbors who had originally been antagonistic were now attending the meetings. The highlight of Alice's return was witnessing the baptism of one of the boys from the Sunday school class. In December 1916, three young men were baptized as a direct result of Alice's teaching.

Alice was made an honorary lifetime member of the Christian Woman's Board of Missions but worked in Japan independent of any society. She received most of her support from the Broadway Church of Christ in Los Angeles and B. F. Coulter. The Broadway church was not satisfied with the growth of the Sendagaya church however, and following Coulter's death they yielded their charge to McCaleb. Under his direction, and with Alice's help, they reported three baptisms in February 1919 and another two in March. Alice also supported a young Japanese man, Tetsuji Kochi, in a Bible training school. Kochi conducted the weekly evangelistic meetings in her school. The Sendagaya church remained a cappella until 1921 when the Japanese members chose to add instruments.

A Disastrous Earthquake

On September 1, 1923, Japan suffered the most severe natural disaster in her history. An earthquake measuring between 7.9 and 8.4 on the Richter scale, with the epicenter just offshore from the port of Yokohama in Sagami Bay, destroyed three-fourths of Tokyo and practically all of Yokohama within thirty seconds. The ground dropped vertically three feet, cracks opened in the earth large enough for a car to disappear into, and the concrete seawall swung back and forth like a gate before collapsing into the sea. Within ten minutes, the streets of Tokyo were ten inches deep in water. Fires erupted and burned for two days, consuming what was still standing after the initial shock. At least ten thousand people crammed into flooded Yokohama Park, thus saving them from the fires that surrounded the park as they lay in the water and covered their faces with mud. Over 105,000 were reported dead and 35,000 more missing. Some had been buried in landslides while others were carried away in tidal waves. Thousands more were injured and over 1.5 million were left homeless. Many of the refugees were taken in by churches and schools in the surrounding towns including those operated by the Restoration missionaries. The missionaries also lost much of their personal belongings—clothing and household goods—in the fires that followed the quake.

Alice was in Tokyo during the quake but found refuge on the back lot of her home. For sometime afterward, she lived in a booth made of mats until a new house could be obtained. Moving to the Zoshigaya area of Tokyo, she had a house built with the lower level again used as the church meeting place equipped with such amenities as a baptistery and two small classrooms in addition to the kitchen and dining room. As in Sendagaya, her living quarters were upstairs.

Alice died in Japan on March 5, 1928, during an influenza epidemic and is buried in the Zoshigaya Cemetery in Tokyo. For several years prior to her death, she had been in poor health, likely the result of a stroke; descriptions indicate she had suffered a complete loss of memory and had trouble with her arm rendering her unable to care for herself. Her faithful Japanese orphan, Masai Kurachi, whom she had adopted and trained as her "Bible woman" many years before, took care of her.

Because of the large population in Tokyo, cemetery space is hard to come by, and most of the deceased are cremated with only a small grave marker placed in the cemetery to record their life and death. The municipal government owns the cemetery, and the families of those buried there must pay a yearly fee to maintain the grave marker. If no one pays the fee, the gravestone is removed along with any record of the deceased. Kurachi paid the yearly fee for Alice Miller's gravestone for over fifty years. In more recent years, Japanese Christians erected a large monument in honor of Alice.

Alice was one of the most modest missionaries among those in Japan. She rarely sent reports to be printed in the Christian journals. When she did, they were regarding the work being done and self-effacing to the degree that she even requested at times that her name not be used. The *Christian Standard* stated in November 1911 that her salary was spent mostly for the work and for charity while her own living expenses amounted to about ten dollars per month. The article concluded, "This noble woman deserves the highest honor from the church of Christ as one of His most self-denying and faithful workers."

CHAPTER FOUR

CALLA AND KATE: TWO HOOSIER TEACHERS

In November 1885, Charles and Laura Garst wrote home begging for more single women to join the work in Japan. Calla Harrison and Kate V. Johnson responded to their request. Kate said her decision was made as a result of reading earnest appeals made in the *Christian Standard* for single lady missionaries. The two women had been schoolteachers in Madison, Indiana. When they volunteered to be missionaries, the Foreign Christian Missionary Society sent them in 1886 to Akita, Japan.

Laura Garst described their first meeting as less than impressive. "I can't tell you how funny they did look to us in the tall hats in vogue in 1886," she wrote in her biography of her husband. "The young ladies were pronounced blondes, the first the Akita people had seen, and there were many discussions as to whether their hair might be a new kind of gray hair. . . . the vari-colored hair and eyes of the foreigner impresses them as most extraordinary."

In Akita, the women were welcomed by pioneer missionary George T. Smith and his new wife Candace Lhamon. Following the death on the mission field of his first wife Josephine, Smith returned to the States and married Candace a year later. Within four years, the Society moved Calla from Akita to Tokyo when it was thought the missionaries could have greater results in the capital city. Kate was relocated to Shonai.

Calla, born in 1859 in North Madison, Indiana, was the first woman to graduate from Hanover College. She had been baptized in Indiana when she was fourteen. In Japan, she was a tireless worker although she was in poor health, a common occurrence among Western missionaries. The climate and paper-thin houses took a toll on nearly every westerner. Tuberculosis also ran rampant.

Around 1892, Calla severed her ties with the Society and began working independently. She helped establish the first Church of Christ in Japan at Yotsuya while working with Lucia Scott and Carme Hostetter.

Calla Harrison
Photo courtesy of Disciples of Christ Historical Society

In one annual account of her work, Calla reported she taught two and one-h.
hours a day in the day school and two and one-half hours a week in a night school,
conducted three Sunday schools with an average attendance of 220, had charge of
two day schools with an attendance of 40, led two daily prayer meetings, a women's
meeting every Thursday, and a Bible class every Saturday. She was the president of
a Reform Society that had 22 members, and she spent two hours a day studying the
language. She also adopted a young Japanese girl and cared for her. Still, she managed
to make one hundred calls over the course of the year in various Japanese homes.

Calla's busy schedule was necessary given the cultural obstacles missionaries to
Japan faced. For example, the missionaries found it challenging to convince Japanese
converts to relinquish the religions of their ancestors. One of Calla's students wept
with anguish at the thought of destroying her tablets for the dead on the family god-
shelf. On these, a Buddhist priest had written the posthumous name of the dead.
"The idols are no longer anything to me," the woman explained, "but these, *these*! I
have been taught from childhood that in these reside the spirits of my loved dead.
What shall I do? I cannot burn them!" Calla advised her to bury the tablets, which she
was willing to do, and she became a Christian.

Another obstacle that often stood in the way of Japanese women converting to
Christianity was the practice of families selling their daughters. Daughters were considered a burden. When a family could not afford to raise a girl, they found willing
buyers in the brothels of Tokyo. On one such occasion, Calla was asked to visit a poor
girl who was dying and in distress over her life of shame. The girl had been sold into
prostitution when very young but knew enough about Christianity to know that this
behavior was not acceptable. On the other hand, she also adhered to the virtue of
honoring her parents who had arranged this lifestyle for her.

A Buddhist priest advised her simply not to think about it. Calla offered her the
peace of Christ's words to the woman taken in adultery: "Neither do I condemn thee,
go and sin no more." Such encounters motivated the young missionaries to find ways
to prevent the young women from being forced into such a lifestyle in the first place
and most women missionaries in the Restoration Movement rescued numerous girls,
taking them into their own homes to live and train for more inviolable occupations.

HEALTH FORCES RELOCATION

After seven years in Japan, Calla's health began to deteriorate due to the harsh weather conditions and she took a furlough to the States in 1893. On December 4, 1894, she set sail for the Land of the Rising Sun once again from San Francisco on the *S.S. Oceanic*, traveling in the company of Alice Miller who was about to begin her ministry in Japan. Calla disembarked in Hawaii where she worked for ten months among the Japanese living there. She then continued to Japan and worked with the church at Ashikaga but was still unable to cope with the weather. Within two years, she left Japan to regain her health in Southern California. In Los Angeles, probably on the recommendation of Alice Miller, she connected with the Broadway Church of Christ where B. F. Coulter was the minister.

Calla spent 1899 as the State Organizer in Kansas, touring the state to increase interest in foreign missions. Before sailing back to Hawaii that summer, she visited the headquarters of *Missionary Tidings,* the official publication of the Christian Woman's Board of Missions, in Indiana with her adopted Japanese daughter Cora. When she reached Hawaii, she found Alice Miller resting there while waiting to bid bon voyage to Kate Johnson who was heading home on furlough.

B. F. Coulter had visited Japan a number of years previously and brought a young man back with him who had become a good friend of Coulter's son, Frank. Fukuda began bringing his Japanese friends living in Los Angeles to the Coulter's house and the Broadway Church of Christ. They had an interest in the Bible and requested an English Bible class to learn more about this "American religion." The group began meeting in the church basement on Sunday afternoons.

By 1903, Calla was back in Los Angeles and Coulter invited her to take charge of the English Bible class. She spent the next nine years in Los Angeles where she assisted in the evangelization of Japanese in the United States. The work in Japan was still a priority for her and, aware of their constant need for financial assistance, she wrote to Cunningham in 1905, explaining that since her support in Los Angeles was being provided by the Broadway Church of Christ, she would recommend that her previous donors direct their gifts to him.

Calla was not only interested in teaching Fukuda and his friends, but she also wanted to reach their wives and children who were adjusting to a new country. Gradually, classes for women were added with instruction in sewing and cooking as well as English, and they established a kindergarten for the children. It was from this simple beginning that the Japanese Christian Institute in Los Angeles emerged. It later became known as All People's Church and Community Center.

The 1910 census lists Calla as a widow although there is no evidence that she was ever married. The presence of her adopted Japanese daughter, Cora, may have prompted the census taker to write "widowed" as her marital status. In 1912, she moved to Hawaii once more where she remained until 1933, working among the Japanese on the Islands as a teacher and interpreter with Cora assisting her. Even during this time, her heart was with the work in Japan as she occasionally sent financial gifts to those still laboring in the Sunrise Kingdom. Sadly, Cora died in 1922 but Calla continued her work in Hawaii. She made her home with friends in Kansas for a brief time after 1933 but lived the rest of her life in Hawaii until her death July 5, 1937. She was buried in Honolulu by the side of her adopted daughter.

An Influential Teacher

In the July 1886 edition of the *Indiana School Journal*, it was reported concerning Kate V. Johnson that "one of Madison's most efficient teachers has gone to Japan." She would prove to be an efficient teacher there as well.

Kate Johnson was born in St. Louis, Missouri, November 5, 1860. Following graduation from the National Normal School in Madison, Indiana, she taught in the Madison public school system. She arrived in Japan in July 1886 with Calla Harrison. The Foreign Christian Missionary Society claims her as their second-longest-serving missionary. However, she actually resigned from the Society in 1906 in order to take over the work temporarily left vacant by Alice Miller's departure. Cunningham, who had taken over the supervision of the Yotsuya Mission, commented that with Kate's twenty years of experience and "aptness for mission work, Miss Johnson fills Miss Miller's place as few missionaries could do." Kate and Alice also shared living quarters for a time and usually hosted the annual Christmas party in their home.

Kate wrote of her work that year, "I have endeavored to carry on the work she [Alice Miller] had charge of and take care of my ten girls. One of my girls is now capable of giving music lessons to the other children." She noted the Christmas celebration at which all the children had been given shawls, mufflers, mittens, shoes, stockings, slates, New Testaments, Christmas cards, cakes, candy, and oranges. Such generosity was typically made possible by a "good sized check" from B. F. Coulter.

She mentioned that the parents had all been given cakes, candy, oranges, and a cake of Ivory soap. This particular brand of soap resulted in an unexpected gift for Kate's mission. One of the waifs Kate had taken into her home eventually grew into a reliable and trusted helper. When Kate left on furlough, she left this young girl, Naoe san, with the supplies necessary to sustain herself by baking bread and making jelly to sell in a little roadside shop.

While waiting in Yokohama for her ship to sail, Kate received a note from Naoe with two yen enclosed, the equivalent of one U.S. dollar, requesting that Kate send her two yen's worth of Ivory soap—the only soap she was familiar with—for she "could not live without Ivory soap!" When Kate told her supporters in the States of Naoe's transformed life, she mentioned her request for Ivory soap. Unknown to Kate, several of the deacons and elders in the church where she spoke were manufacturers of Ivory soap. The next day, she received a gift of ten dollars from one of these men directing it specifically to Naoe. Kate immediately sent it to the young girl who received it on the very day that her father died. Naoe had not known how she was going to pay his funeral expenses until the unexpected money arrived.

During the Russo-Japanese War, Kate taught a course for nurses every Sunday. She also hosted a Bible lesson in her home every morning. She spoke to the women's club about hygiene, care of children, cooking, and other domestic matters. She visited the women in their homes and received visits from them.

Attempting to transcend the differences between the pro-Society and anti-Society Christians, she wrote in the Society's paper, "The school, the S. [Sunday] Schools, the church, and the children in our home, are as much your work as mine. We are

Kate V. Johnson
Photo courtesy Disciples of Christ Historical Society

all workers together with Him whose word shall not return unto him void; workers together with Him who is not willing that any should perish, but that all should come to repentance."

RECONNECTED TO THE SOCIETY

Apparently Kate's efforts to maintain a favorable relationship with the Society worked. When Alice Miller returned to her station November 5, 1907, Kate went back to her work under the Society, retiring in 1917 on a modest pension supplied by the Society. During the remaining two years of her life, she spoke frequently to churches, Sunday schools, and Christian Endeavor Societies.

While in Japan she conducted a charity school, held meetings for women, taught Bible classes, and went out on tours of outlying towns. On one occasion, she spent forty-six days visiting distant outposts and teaching hundreds who had never heard the gospel before. In one place, opposition to Christianity was still so rampant that public meetings could not be held. Not to be deterred, Kate taught in secret and some months later learned that one of her students had walked twenty-five miles to find a minister who would baptize him.

Her work began in Akita but she was stationed by the Society in Shonai in 1888. A year later she was transferred to Tsurugaoka to assist Laura Garst. The following year, she was relocated in Tokyo. Wherever she was stationed, she kept busy in evangelistic work. In one year, she reported having held seventy meetings for women, and fifty-two Sunday school services. She taught two hours a day in the English school and thirty minutes a day in the night school for two months. She had charge of a Japanese school of forty-two students which took three hours a week and she made 130 house calls and spent the remainder of her time studying the language.

She also opened her home to young girls to whom she taught the finer things of life as well as the Bible. When a local magazine editor interviewed her, he told her he was not interested in the Bible or its teachings and he saw no need to instruct women in such things. Kate called in several of the girls who were living with her and asked them to repeat Proverbs 31:10-31 for the interviewer. He was pleased with the description of the ideal wife and asked who had written it. Kate informed him that an Oriental King named Solomon was the supposed author. Satisfied, he asked for a copy to include in his article and subsequently published a portion of the Scriptures in spite of his proclaimed disregard for them.

Kate was described as deeply religious, highly cultured, and possessing a charming personality. "Miss Johnson was indeed richly endowed for the life work to which she was called and carried out so successfully to its finish," read her obituary in *World Call*.

Her greatest accomplishment, however, may have been the influence she had on one other person—Adele Shepherd. Adele had been one of her students in Madison before Kate went to Japan. Adele was ten years old when her family moved to Madison, and she spent the next five years under Kate's influence and tutelage. Only nine years separated them in age, and a strong bond of friendship developed between pupil and student.

Adele's family moved to Nashville two years before Kate sailed for Japan. They maintained contact during Kate's years overseas, and there is evidence that Adele may have contributed financially to Kate's work for several years. When Kate returned home on furlough in 1904, she spent time in Adele's home. Her friendship with the young Shepherd girl instilled Adele's yearning to be a missionary to Japan also. However, God had other plans for Adele. She married Will Andrews and raised a family in Dickson, Tennessee. Instead, she passed her interest in Japan and her desire to go as a missionary on to one of her children—her daughter Sarah Andrews, whom we will meet later.

Loduska Wirick

Photo courtesy of Disciples of Christ Historical Society

CHAPTER FIVE

LODUSKA WIRICK: NIGHTINGALE OF THE ORIENT

In 1890, a thirty-two-year-old single woman arrived in Japan as a semi-independent missionary. Belle Bennett, a student at Drake University and the daughter of missionaries serving in Australia, was scheduled to depart for Japan in May 1889. However, the day before she was due to leave she drowned in the Des Moines River in a boating accident. Students at Drake University raised four thousand dollars in her memory and requested a volunteer to go in her place. A fellow student, Loduska Wirick, volunteered to take her place.

From Tipton, Iowa, Loduska was the third child of fifteen born to Joseph and Sarah Wirick. At Drake University, where she studied medicine, she was the librarian for the literary society, The Athenian. For several years she taught in the Iowa Industrial School for Girls in Mitchellville before returning to Drake to complete her education. With seven large trunks, she sailed for Japan in July 1890.

"You Shall Hear of My Joy"

The Young Ladies' Missionary Society of University Place at Drake, who had organized the Belle Bennett fund, followed her progress. As Loduska bid them farewell, she told them, "I am only a drop in the bucket. One is not missed by the many. I do not grieve for this. You shall hear of my joy, but the sorrows and sickness, the heartache and weariness will be told only to the Father. In His name I go forth gladly, and even martyrdom is nothing compared with what the Master suffered for me. Hoping we may meet again here, if not we all know where the reunion will be for eternity."

She encountered her first heartache even before reaching the west coast of the United States. In Denver, she received a telegram informing her that her brother in Leadville was deathly ill with brain fever, but a washout prevented her from going to see him. Evidence suggests he survived the illness, and she continued on her journey, sailing on the steamship *S.S. China* on July 30.

Although not officially under the auspices of the Missionary Society, she worked closely with others from the Society and continued to receive part of her support from the group at Drake University. During her first five years on the field, the Foreign Christian Missionary Society controlled the Belle Bennett fund, and it was only after that time that she was able to receive the proceeds directly and be totally independent. Her primary source of income was directly from churches and individuals who kept her supplied with the necessities of life.

She was overjoyed when she learned that Azbill and his group of missionaries were coming as independent workers without ties to a missionary society. She told J. M. McCaleb, "The Lord will never let you suffer. Money doesn't give me the least concern. I am not a bit afraid but that I will be supported."

McCaleb reported meeting her on his first Sunday in Japan in 1892. She was living with Eugene and Mattie Snodgrass (a husband and wife team who had come to Japan in 1888) and helping with their church work at Daimon-cho in the Koishikawa Ward. The children in her Sunday school sang "Bringing in the Sheaves" in Japanese for McCaleb's enjoyment.

Loduska worked among the women of Tokyo and conducted a Sunday school for the children. Although single, she became a substitute mother to several Japanese girls and at one time had eleven orphan girls living with her. Another time, a thief broke into her house only to discover about fifteen young girls sleeping on the floor and nothing worth stealing—only a kettle for cooking and a small charcoal-burning heater.

She was active in the rescue work of the Women's Christian Temperance Union and paid for a subscription of three hundred copies per month of the temperance paper, *Kuni no Hikari* (Light of Our Land). She was a regular visitor to the leper hospital where she spent an entire day twice each month teaching, singing, and helping these isolated people accept their illness. Even as she traveled to and from the hospital, she handed out religious tracts she had written.

When fellow missionary William J. Bishop's wife died in 1900—within a year of their arrival in Japan—he found himself with considerable expenses and without the funds to pay them. He went to Loduska, who handed him her bankbook and told him to withdraw whatever he needed. Her generosity extended to others whether they were supported by the Society or worked as independents. She encouraged Cunningham in his work at Yotsuya, sending a financial contribution while she was home on furlough in 1903 along with the note, "All work of the Lord is dear to my heart and yours is a part of His."

Seeing the need for a suitable place to conduct worship, she had one of her brothers, Thomas, who was a carpenter, draw up plans for a chapel that would seat three hundred. When it was dedicated on March 14, 1894, she named it Drake Chapel in honor of her alma mater. In 1897, she donated the chapel building to the Church of Christ and it became the Koishikawa Church of Christ. It served the church until a B-29 bombing raid destroyed it during World War II.

Loduska took a year furlough in 1895 for an additional year of training at Drake. Back in Japan, she continued teaching English classes in several schools including the Peer School, Keio University, and the Gakushuin Noble School, where the most promising young men of Japan and children of the nation's leaders received their education.

When McCaleb went on furlough in 1899, Loduska took over his school for the poor and conducted it until his return. She told him when he returned in September 1901 that the day he landed in Yokohama was the first cool day since summer had set in. The high humidity and temperatures in Tokyo during the summers could be unbearable.

WORK AMONG THE SOLDIERS

The Japanese dearly loved Loduska for her compassionate work, especially among the soldiers during the Russo-Japanese war of 1904-1905. She became known as the

Loduska Wirick is transported in a traditional jinrikisha
Photo courtesy of Disciples of Christ Historical Society

Angel of the Hospital and the Nightingale of the Orient as she worked among four military hospitals in Tokyo. On one of her visits to the military hospital at Toyama, which cared for seven thousand patients just two blocks from her home, she made the acquaintance of a soldier named Yoshimasu whose face had been crushed and whose eyesight had been destroyed by a bursting shell. He was so depressed that he had attempted suicide but failed. He could not face returning to his wife and three-month-old daughter, whom he had never seen. Loduska went to the school for the blind, learned Braille and taught it to Yoshimasu using the Gospel of John. Other patients became interested and took turns reading to the blind soldier. Within four months, twenty-five of those patients, including Yoshimasu, had become Christians.

Encouraged by Loduska, the young man attended the school for the blind and with her help translated four hundred hymns into Braille. Not content to stop there, he asked Loduska to teach him the tunes he didn't know. As a guest in her home for nearly two weeks, he learned the songs from her, nearly singing himself hoarse in the process. It was reported that there were days when her house was filled with blind men for the whole day while she told them about Christ, sang with them, and taught them to sing.

Yoshimasu was not the only soldier who heard the gospel story from Loduska. Following the Russo-Japanese war she maintained correspondence with thousands of soldiers scattered over Japan, Manchuria, Korea, and Hawaii. Many of them organized Bible classes, and their students became her correspondents as well. Once she received a postcard simply addressed, "Wirick San, Tokyo." In a city of two million people, she was known so well, the card reached her. The card read, "Please send me the book that says, 'Come unto me, all ye who are weary and heavy-laden, and I will give you rest.'" Among her possessions when she died were over eight thousand letters from people all over the Orient requesting the "I Shall Give You Rest" book. The University Place Church of Des Moines assisted her with money for stationery and postage.

Even she did not know how far her influence extended. Once while she was speaking at a meeting, a soldier saluted her. When she did not recognize him, he explained that she had laid a Gospel of John on his pillow when he was in the hospital. Later he became a Christian. Others including doctors and students formed Bible classes as a result of her work among the sick. Even the families of those she had ministered to revered her and placed her picture on the "god-shelf" in their Buddhist and Shinto homes.

The Christian paper *World Call* reported that "fishermen, railway workers, doctors, blind men, the lepers, all knew her for their friend." She was honored by Emperor Meiji when he presented her with three or more silver loving cups and the government gave her a medal in recognition of her work with the wounded service men.

FINAL FURLOUGH

Loduska came home to the States on furlough again in 1913 only to be told by doctors at the Mayo Clinic that she had terminal cancer. "This life which has been given by God is short," she said, "but I would like to continue the work entrusted to me by God." She immediately bid farewell to her aging mother and made arrangements to return to Japan to conclude her work among those whom she loved so much, arriving April 23, 1913. Loduska died in Tokyo a year later on April 30, 1914. J. M. McCaleb conducted her funeral in the Koishikawa church which was attended by over 500 people, including nearly 250 students from one of her schools. Special music was rendered by a quartet composed of Marie McCoy, Stella Walker Young, J. M. McCaleb and W. D. Cunningham. McCaleb reported in the *Missionary Messenger* that "Mr. Ando and Mr. Nemoto, the latter a member of parliament, and both of national reputation as temperance workers, attended her funeral and made speeches." Tadashi Nemoto had been led to faith by Loduska, after which he initiated the law prohibiting drinking and smoking among minors. Taro Ando was the former counsel to Hawaii.

Loduska Wirick's tombstone in Tokyo
Photo courtesy of Yukikazu Obata

Others who spoke at her funeral included one of her Japanese converts who became a minister, a representative from the Leper Home which she regularly visited, a young boy representing the Sunday school which met in her home, and a representative of the president of the school where she taught. In addition telegrams were read from several friends.

Many newspaper articles were written about her from Des Moines, Iowa, to Japan. *The Tipton Iowa Advertiser* carried her obituary on May 8, 1914. The *Leedy Chronicle* and the *Record of Christian Work* also printed extensive articles about her career. *The Youths Companion*, a weekly for young people, carried a eulogy in March 1915. One of the three largest daily papers in Japan, *The Mainichi*, remembered her work nearly seventy years after her death with a feature article published March 20, 1983, titled, "Miss Nightingale of Orient." In response, *The Tipton Conservative* published an article recounting her life also.

She was buried in the Foreigner's Section of the Somei Cemetery in Tokyo. Because of her prominence and recognition by Emperor Meiji, her gravestone will be maintained without the yearly fee to the municipal government. Over her grave is a stone pedestal supporting an open Bible. The inscription in Japanese on the left hand page of the book contains a portion of Hebrews 11:4—"And by it he being dead, yet speaketh."

CHAPTER SIX

MARY AND LAVINIA: AN INTERNATIONAL FRIENDSHIP

In the same year that Azbill's first group of missionaries entered Japan, two other single women arrived under the sponsorship of two different missionary societies. Lavinia Oldham was sent by the Foreign Christian Missionary Society and Mary Rioch was sent by the Christian Woman's Board of Missions, both organizations of the Christian Church. Mary was a native of Canada and it was the women's missionary society of her home congregation in Ontario that sent her to Japan in November 1892. Lavinia Oldham sailed on the same ship. When the two met on board the ship, a friendship began that lasted more than thirty years. The two women rented a house together in Tokyo and began reaching out to the Japanese people.

Mary Rioch was from a "missionary family." Her mother was a leader of the Christian Woman's Board of Missions in Hamilton, Ontario, and her brother David answered a call to take the gospel to India. Mary's own call to the mission field came about two years after she graduated from the Toronto Normal School. She admitted having interest in missions even as a child and often thought about the sacrifices missionaries were called to make. The Ontario Christian Woman's Board of Missions was interested in sending someone to a foreign field and had requested the Foreign Christian Missionary Society to suggest someone.

One day Mary seemed to sense a voice asking her, "Why don't you go?" She tried to put the thought out of her mind, but the question would not go away. After a week of wrestling with herself over the answer, she concluded that she had no excuse not to go. She approached her mother with her decision. "She turned white when I told her," Mary wrote, "got up and looked out of the window for a long time, then she turned to me and said, 'I am glad. I always hoped one of my children would go, but I had not thought of it being you.'"

Mary applied to the Ontario Woman's Mission Board hoping to be sent to China as a nurse. The Ontario group, however, was not sure they would be able to sustain someone in the field on their own efforts, so they requested the Maritime Provinces Woman's Mission Board to join with them in the effort. This group of women had a special interest in Japan, as Josephine Smith, who had died in Japan, was from the Maritimes. They agreed to assist in Mary's support provided she was sent to Japan. She arrived in Yokohama on November 3, 1892.

For the first few months, Mary and her new friend Lavinia moved in with another single woman—Calla Harrison. Calla had eight or nine Japanese girls living in her home, the nucleus of a girls' school, but she made room for the two new missionaries. Mary at once joined in teaching the girls English.

Calla also had a preaching service in her home every Sunday morning and observed the Lord's Supper. The preacher was a young man Calla was educating who was attending Presbyterian Divinity College. He was a convert of her work in Akita. From this small start emerged the Koishikawa church that met in Loduska Wirick's chapel beginning in 1897.

THE NEED FOR A SCHOOL

Everywhere Mary and Lavinia walked in their neighborhood they were followed by a large group of children. Calla explained to Mary why there were so many children on the streets during school hours. The government did not provide education for all children and what was available was not free. Most of the families in the slum area where they set up housekeeping were too poor to pay the tuition or buy the necessary school supplies. Others were not permitted to attend the government schools because their births had not been registered. Calla encouraged Mary to rent a house in the middle of the slum and start a Sunday school.

Every Sunday Calla sent two of the Japanese girls she was caring for to Mary's house to teach. Mary and Lavinia wrote the words to the hymns in large letters on white paper but were dismayed when they realized that none of the children could read even the simplest words. The need for a day school and kindergarten was obvious.

The following spring, Mary and Lavinia rented a dainty Japanese house in a new area. High bamboo groves and evergreen hedges hemmed them in and hid the fact that their house was surrounded by Buddhist temples and priests' homes. The two women were often stoned, and vile placards were posted on their gates at night.

Mary Rioch Miller
Photo courtesy of Disciples of Christ Historical Society

Their sleep was interrupted by the temple drums and chanting priests. Many times their work was halted.

On the positive side, they were also near the first Christian college for boys in the empire. Soon they had a request to begin an English Bible class for the young men who wanted to practice their English. Feeling the purpose of their mission in Japan was to reach the women and children, they were reluctant to grant the request. However, after praying about it, they felt they could not refuse. Within six years, before the women's first furlough home, every young man in the class had become a Christian.

Throughout her career in Japan, Lavinia continued this class for young college men, who regarded her as a mother-figure. As a result of her work, several of her students entered the ministry as preachers, teachers, and evangelists among their fellow Japanese. A married missionary in Japan, Myrtle Hagin, stated that until their preaching schools began, Lavinia put more men into the ministry than any other missionary.

Lavinia's and Mary's charity school was crude at best. They used low benches for desks with the children squatting on the floor. They had a blackboard and some chalk. The children had to furnish their own books, slates, pencils, pens, brushes, and old newspapers to write on.

The children who came to their school were from very poor homes with large families. Frequently the older children, left in charge of their younger siblings, would arrive for school with a baby tied on their back, the customary mode for carrying infants. The presence of several babies did not create a very educational atmosphere, and Lavinia and Mary found it necessary to insist that their students secure other care for their young siblings. With the help of a "Bible woman" they were able to establish some discipline, and learning began to take place.

A "Bible woman" was a native who was able to speak English and knew the Bible sufficiently to have embraced Christianity. They were trained to teach the Bible, call in homes, conduct meetings for women, lead in song, teach Sunday school classes, and, if necessary, lead in church service. Most missionaries, men and women, employed a Bible woman. The men found it helpful to have a woman who could enter Japanese homes to study with the wives of the men they were teaching, as it was imprudent for a man to study with a woman.

In fact, the plight of women in Japan at the time was abasing. On those rare occasions when they went out in public with their husbands, they walked behind him two or three steps. This rule applied even when entering cars, trains, or rooms. Men could divorce their wives for adultery, but women could not do the same with an unfaithful husband. Women were not allowed to hear a political speech, and had such low self-esteem that they never looked anyone in the eye. Many still practiced the custom of shaving their eyebrows and blackening their teeth when married in order to make themselves unattractive to other men. They worked in the fields and in the homes, and they bore and cared for the children. And they were generally uneducated. Christianity helped bring a new sense of worth to Japanese women and elevated them to a respectable position in their culture.

Mary's and Lavinia's charity school began as a morning program since the children were required to work the rest of the day. In this part of the city, the children's work was at home, out of which their parents operated small factories. Each week, men delivered work in small carts and distributed it to families. They returned at the end of the week to collect the finished products. Some of the older children worked in a tobacco factory earning a few cents per day.

Mary and Lavinia began meeting with the mothers of their students once a week to instruct them in nutrition, cooking, sewing, reading, and Christianity. These meetings became so popular that they didn't stop even when school was dismissed for summer vacation.

THE MARY RIOCH KINDERGARTEN

The school flourished, and another teacher was hired. The building became too small to contain them all, so they found a larger house, but soon they had to remodel it to make larger rooms to accommodate their increasing number of students. They also had to hire a resident caretaker—a necessity in case of fire. Since Japanese houses were constructed of paper walls with sliding paper partitions separating rooms, fire was a very real danger.

Although started as a half-day charity school for the poor with no tuition charged, they soon added a small fee, and then expanded to an all-day school with a slightly higher fee. They found the Japanese to be proud people who did not like charity and preferred to pay for what they received. Other missionaries found this true, also, and they learned they got a better response when they sold Bibles and tracts for a small fee than when they handed them out for free.

Around 1906, Mary received funds from the Missionary Society to build a larger, two-story house. It was dedicated September 12, 1908. This provided so much room that she decided to start a kindergarten. She reported 1908 as the happiest year of her time in Japan. In 1911, fire claimed the building, but she had acted on advice to insure the building so it was rebuilt, better than before. When Mary left Japan in 1916, the school had enlarged to include a six-year course of study, and there were five large rooms filled to capacity, accommodating 275 students. Another 45 students attended the kindergarten. The Bible was taught daily to all students, and they received a special Sunday school session once a week. Many years after Mary's retirement, the school continued to exist and was known as the Mary Rioch Kindergarten.

Mary's work in Japan also included providing a home for several young girls and overseeing a church. This was an extension of the work begun by Calla Harrison. Less than a year after Mary and Lavinia arrived in Japan, Calla went home on furlough leaving them in charge of her girls and the church meeting in her home. The weekly preaching and Lord's Supper continued to be conducted by the man Calla had arranged for, but when all their male colleagues were in the States on furlough for nearly two years, Mary oversaw all the work of the church.

Loduska Wirick also aided in the growth of this church, as the large chapel she had built was about two blocks from Mary's school. When Calla's house-church outgrew the house, they began meeting in Loduska's chapel. This eventually grew into the Koishikawa church, one of the largest churches among the Restoration Movement in the city.

During her spare time, Mary taught an English Bible class in the Formosa University and another in the Waseda University, and she established a second day school and kindergarten in another part of the city. Like other Westerners in Japan, Mary and Lavinia sought relief from the hot, humid summers in the city by retreating to the mountains. In 1910, however, they were forced back to Tokyo when a typhoon swept

Lavinia Oldham
Photo courtesy of Disciples of Christ Historical Society

through their mountain home. They were carried out of the house at two o'clock in the morning and spent the rest of the summer with the Cunninghams.

In 1915, Mary married a missionary from California, George Miller, and returned to America. She died December 10, 1957, in her hometown of Hamilton, Ontario, Canada.

THE HOSPITABLE STORYTELLER

Lavinia was remembered as a wonderful storyteller especially adept at relating the account of the cross. On one occasion, an elderly man in one of her classes was so touched by Lavinia's narration that he put his head down on the table and began to weep. "Why hasn't someone told me this long ago?" he cried. "I did not know before that anyone had died for me, and here I am, an old man with only a few more years to serve Him in return for all this."

Lavinia, a graduate of Daughters' College in Harrodsburg, Kentucky, had been a public school teacher for twenty years in her native state before making the decision to go to Japan. She worked side-by-side with Mary Rioch in providing a home for many homeless girls. She was uplifted to see some of the children she had taken in and trained grow up, marry, and take over some of the work in the schools and churches. Besides her work with Mary, Lavinia conducted three Sunday schools, two charity schools, two women's Bible meetings each week, and an English Bible class. When she received an inheritance from her family in Kentucky, she used the money to build a chapel near her house in the Ushigome Ward. She used some of the funds to build summer homes in Karuizawa that she rented out for supplemental income. Deriving from this revenue, she responded to many benevolent needs encountered in her work in Tokyo, including assisting some of the other missionaries when their funds ran low. She also gave generously from the savings she had accumulated from her years of teaching before coming to Japan.

Hospitality was definitely one of her gifts as she opened her home, not only to the local girls she taught, but also to other missionaries during times of need. When Loduska Wirick was nearing the end of her life, it was Lavinia who stayed by her side ministering to her and caring for her to the end. Lavinia's co-workers reported the highlights of each year being the annual gatherings of their fellow missionaries at Lavinia's home for traditional Thanksgiving and Christmas dinners. Christmas of 1906 included a smoked ham Lavinia brought from Kentucky when she returned from furlough, and the next year the ham was supplied by Jessie Asbury, another young single missionary, who brought it from Kentucky as a gift for Lavinia.

Fund-raising was another of Lavinia's gifts. While home on furlough in 1904 to 1905, she raised two thousand dollars within ten minutes at a meeting in St. Louis. It was claimed if she had had thirty minutes she could have raised ten thousand dollars.

When her health began to fail in 1921, she retired from the mission field and returned to her Kentucky home on the pension supplied by the Missionary Society. She died June 26, 1927, in Lexington, Kentucky, and is buried in the cemetery at Mount Sterling.

Rose Armbruster

Photo courtesy Disciples of Christ Historical Society

CHAPTER SEVEN

ROSE ARMBRUSTER: ENERGETIC EVANGELIST

R ose Armbruster was sent to Japan by the Foreign Christian Missionary Soci-
ety in 1903. She remained for nearly thirty years. Born in Springfield, Illinois,
she was a serious student and became a public school teacher after graduating from
Hiram College. She spent her first furlough at the Bible Teachers' Training School in
New York and while home on her second furlough did graduate study at Columbia
University in New York.

A Gifted Evangelist

Rose had a gift for language and quickly learned not only to speak Japanese but
also to read and write it. After a short assignment in Tokyo where she lived temporarily with Mary Rioch, she was stationed in Akita where she continued until 1919.
She organized a city Sunday School Association in Akita and served as its president.
Her report for June that year stated that she had attended thirty-three church meetings during the month with a total attendance of 779, taught eighteen people in her
home, conducted three Sunday schools per week, and made four calls in homes to
teach. This was a typical schedule for Rose as another report in January 1920 revealed

thirty meetings, ten Bible studies in her home, and seventeen in Japanese homes during the previous month.

When she first arrived in Japan, she was impressed that so much work could be accomplished with so little equipment and such poor buildings. Winters in Akita often included snow. Rose wrote, "One often has to wade through snow almost to the knees, and then sit on the matted floor of a thatched-roofed house—dark these winter days as the outer wooden shutters must be kept closed to keep out the bitter wind. Glass doors have not yet come to Akita except in very rich homes. The only heat is a charcoal fire over which swings the iron tea kettle, and the hot tea served with salt pickle is most comforting."

Her work in Akita was usually conducted in the Josephine Smith Memorial Chapel, built in honor of the first Disciples' missionary to die in Japan. "The church is a queer old building," Rose wrote, "with a wood stove to take off some of the winter chill. It is on the women's side of the room for which I am grateful."

Another time she wrote about a trip she made to one of the outlying areas. "We went by train to the first town, the Bible Woman and I; the next lap over the mountains by jinrikisha and the rest of the way in 'gata-gata-basha' (a sort of omnibus with no springs, drawn by an excuse of a horse) but I walked most of the way. We did about three miles an hour! Over hills, mountains and plains. Were caught in a snowstorm in the highest mountains."

She reported that their routine was to go to the inn, take a hot bath, eat supper, and then go to the church if there was one in the town. If no church had yet been established, then they would hold a meeting in a large room of the inn. The meeting would begin with a children's gathering and then the adults would join. They would sing and teach those in attendance hymns then deliver a message from the Bible. The meeting would conclude at ten o'clock, although many stayed much later to sing more hymns, ask questions, and discuss the problems of living as Christians in a non-Christian environment. Rose and her Bible woman would leave early the next morning to journey on to the next town.

On one occasion they came upon a middle-aged woman who thought Rose must be the husband of the Bible woman, as she had never seen anyone but a man wearing shoes, hat, and spectacles. Rose trained more than one Bible woman in the art of home calls. One of her trainees reported that she "learned from Miss Armbruster that each home call must be a Bible lesson and that one must never leave without offering up a prayer."

Rose described the start of a church in a small town called Otamachi with a population of about ten thousand. "A few of our believers live there and the Japanese pastor from the neighboring city of Mito goes there once a week to hold a service for them. Their leader is a teacher in the Boys' Middle School. Here twenty-nine people were baptized, over half of them students, with several school teachers also. The group met at five o'clock Sunday morning, February 25 [1923], and walked together out to the river, over a mile away, and were baptized. Then they returned to the meeting place and celebrated their first communion service, their faces simply radiating the joy that filled their hearts. At the morning service at ten o'clock, they organized themselves into a Church of Christ, choosing their deacons, covenanting with one another to be true to their Lord and the Master and to labor to build a church in that town."

MORE EVANGELISTIC EFFORTS

As Rose traveled about to assist at evangelistic meetings, she usually rode on the trains third class so she could engage the people in conversation and sow the seed. A third-class ticket provided a straight-backed seat without upholstery at a cost of about $1.10 for a 100-mile trip. On at least one occasion this resulted in a Bible study with a young military officer. The difficult climate of Japan and workload took a toll on Rose, however, and she was forced to return to the States the winter of 1920. "After almost seven months' absence spent in resting and regaining health and strength impaired by overwork last year," she wrote in the spring of 1921, "I returned to Akita in April." During this time she had been blind for four months from overwork. When her health was restored, she returned to Japan and resumed her post in Osaka.

On an evangelistic trip through the Akita district she spent four days in the home of her former Bible woman, Murai san. Six meetings were held in those four days, one of them being for the twenty-five nurses in a large hospital and another in the home of one of the leading Christians who ran a printing plant. As she continued on her journey, two of the Christian women went with her, one of them taking her year-old baby along on her back. At the home where they stayed in the next town, a young Christian man prepared a feast for them consisting of Japanese macaroni with duck and onions, broiled fish, stew, beans, pickles, rice, and cakes, and cocoa for dessert.

In the next village she and Murai san studied with the mayor's wife and daughters. This meeting, held in a hotel, was interrupted by a loud drinking party in the room above them, but the audience paid no attention to the noise. Further on, at the inn in Honjo, she engaged in conversation with an elderly blind man who had never heard about free will. He was gratified to find the answer to many of the questions that had bothered him all of his life.

Back in Tokyo, Rose assisted with the kindergartens and mothers' clubs and taught English in the night school for girls. These English classes prompted her to correspond with Vachel Lindsey, a well-known American poet who was also among the Disciples of Christ.

Rose returned to the States for health reasons again in 1923. She was barely back from her furlough when she was suddenly called Stateside again when her sister-in-law was killed in a car accident. While home, she visited numerous churches, from California to New York and Minnesota to Florida, including African American congregations, to tell the story of mission work in Japan. She sailed for Japan once again in 1926 and found a much-changed Japan from the one she left three years before. City streets were wider and paved with sidewalks in many places. Electric trains had replaced most jinrikishas and the people had begun to wear Western-style clothing and hairstyles. She also noticed a change in the attitude of the people toward the foreigners, no longer regarding them as somewhat superior but more as equals.

She continued her work with two kindergartens and mothers' meetings, making home calls, teaching a cooking class, and teaching two hours a week in the Christy Institute, a business school begun by the missionaries. As the world economy sank in 1929, one of the kindergartens had to be closed for lack of funds. The mothers requested, however, that their Bible class continue, which Rose was glad to do. One mother promised to teach her children to sing the hymns she was learning even though she herself was not yet a Christian.

The mothers' Bible class was a successful evangelistic tool. Rose told of one mother whose homelife had been transformed through the teaching she received. The young woman told Rose she learned to bear the sharp words and opposition of her mother-in-law with quiet patience, and this caused the elder woman to become more gentle and kind, and she no longer opposed her daughter-in-law's attendance at the mothers' meetings and Bible class.

Thanksgiving 1931 afforded an opportunity to give a practical lesson in generosity and the sharing of blessings. The entire preceding week was observed as Thanksgiving Week. Each day, the children brought their gifts of clothing, rice, vegetables, and money. With the aid of the local police, Rose secured a large kitchen near a local park where many homeless people spent the nights. The mothers' Bible class spent several hours preparing and cooking the rice and vegetables then transported them to the distribution point. A local newspaper reporter happened upon the scene, and the Thanksgiving celebration was publicized in all the papers the next day.

In 1932, when funding from the Missionary Society was cut off due to the Depression, Rose came home for the last time. She arrived in Los Angeles on the *Tatsuta Maru* on July 8 and headed for her brother's home in Southern California. She planned to continue east but was delayed when she had an operation at the Mayo Clinic in December. She retired from the Society and recuperated at her sister's home in Denver. She then moved to the California Christian Home in San Gabriel where she died in 1950.

Bertha Clawson
Photo courtesy of Disciples of Christ Historical Society

CHAPTER EIGHT

BERTHA CLAWSON: THE MOST SUCCESSFUL GIRLS' SCHOOL

A co-worker of Rose Armbruster who also spent her final days in the California Christian Home in San Gabriel was Bertha Clawson.

Bertha was the fifth of ten children born to Asa and Rebecca Clawson, who were farmers in Kansas. When she was sixteen, she united with the Methodist Church but upon her father's insistence, she was immersed when she was baptized. This was probably a result of the influence of Bertha's paternal grandmother who was a member of the "Campbellites."

In 1884, soon after her baptism, a typhoid epidemic broke out and Bertha was the first in her family to be stricken. She survived, but both her mother and father died in the same week leaving all ten children orphaned. Bertha was taken in by her father's brother, James Clawson, in Springport, Indiana. Her Uncle James also belonged to the Campbellites, who insisted on only being called "Christians." Bertha considered these Campbellites "queer."

MISSIONARY CALLING

A singing evangelist, while holding a protracted meeting in Springport, suggested that Bertha ought to pursue more formal education at Tri-State Normal School at Angola, Indiana. She took his advice, received her degree in 1896, and began teaching among relatives and friends in Indiana. Later she would do graduate study at Columbia University in New York. But it was at Angola that she came under the influence of more "Campbellites," including Dr. Charles Medbury, a prominent leader of the Disciples of Christ.

During a prayer meeting one night, Medbury proposed that the Angola church ought to support a missionary. As they prayed for guidance, a woman spoke up, "I don't know of anyone we'd rather send than Bertha Clawson." Bertha agreed to their request and applied to the Foreign Christian Missionary Society. After being interviewed in Cincinnati and given a physical exam confirming her good health, the Society decided to send her to Japan. She sailed from San Francisco on March 25, 1898. Kate V. Johnson met her at the dock in Yokohama and took her to a restaurant where she had her first taste of Japanese food.

Bertha's first job was to learn the language. She was then assigned to teach a Sunday school class and help with women's meetings. At the end of her first year in Japan, the governmental restrictions were lifted freeing foreigners to live outside the treaty cities. As a result, Bertha was assigned to assist in the opening of a new work in Osaka, a city with a population of over one million, known as the Pittsburgh of Japan due to its status as the center of manufacturing in the empire. She found the Japanese courteous but sometimes dreaded the home visits. One woman made her granddaughter sprinkle salt on the doorsteps to cleanse them from the foreigners after their visit. The centuries of Buddhism and Shintoism, incorporating ancestor worship and superstitions, were difficult to overcome. There were other disappointments in the work as well.

Bertha agreed to take in a dirty, uncared-for child whose mother was going to sell the young woman into prostitution. Bertha provided a home for the child, gave her singing lessons, and eventually saw her married to a fine young Japanese minister. For several years, things seemed well with the couple. Then one day, the young Japanese bride disappeared and no trace was ever found of her.

Such setbacks did not discourage Bertha, however. She remained optimistic and excited about the work. Upon her return from her first furlough, she wrote back to her family, "A great delight it is to be in Japan once more—Japan, the land of our adoption. . . ." She continued, "Our greatest, our most heartfelt joy has been the glad welcome we have received from our Japanese brothers and sisters and friends. To look into their dear faces, radiant with the light of the gospel of Christ makes one feel that life is well worth living, even though it be lived outside of our own dear America. . . . God grant us long years of service in Japan, if in them we can bring this 'power of God unto salvation,' into the hearts and homes of this people!"

The Girls' School Begins

While home on furlough in 1903, Bertha received a letter from Japan informing her that her fellow missionaries had decided to start a girls' school and they had chosen her to run it. Bertha had no desire to be an educational missionary. She wanted to be evangelistic. She sought the advice of her minister at Angola, Dr. Medbury. "Bertha," he said, "Christian teaching *is* a form of evangelism."

The reasoning for a girls' school hinged on the fact that there was already a boys' school and as Archibald McLean, President of the Foreign Christian Missionary Society pointed out, "to educate one sex and not the other is to defeat the end in view." With a substantial gift from lumber baron R. A. Long, a member of the Disciples of Christ in Kansas, and additional contributions from individuals and churches, twenty thousand dollars was raised to start the school. When Bertha arrived back in Japan in 1904, she began the task of locating a house in which to conduct the school. The first day of class was held on November 4, 1905, in the small parlor of an old home they had rented in Tokyo. She had three full-time teachers and twelve students.

She wrote to Dr. Medbury, "We have just finished the first day of 'Joshi Seigakuin' (girls' religious school). . . . What do you think of this as a prospect for a life's work?" His answer came in the next mail: "I'll tell you what I think of your prospects, I think you are no better than your master. Remember long years ago over in Palestine he started a school for boys, and like you, had just 12, and one teacher. Now that school fills the whole world. Go on with your work and be happy."

Bertha was evangelistic even while directing the school. In the early days of the school, a meeting was held over three nights. On the final night, a weary middle-aged

Bertha Clawson (on far left) with one of her girls' classes
Photo courtesy of Disciples of Christ Historical Society

woman entered and took a seat. At the closing hymn, cards were distributed for those present to indicate a desire to follow Christ or receive further instruction. Inoue san could not sign a card because she could not read or write, but she went to the minister and told him that she wished to become a Christian at once. Bertha was assigned to meet with her for more instruction. She confided to Bertha, "This is the most wonderful story I have ever heard and it is a message that I have been waiting for all my life. I do not want to be an inquirer, I want to make the decision tonight—for I know that I must follow this Christ about whom I have heard tonight." After a few weeks of studying with Bertha she was baptized. Through the following years Bertha continued to mentor her until Inoue san was stricken with cancer. Bertha was at her bedside holding her hand as she passed into the arms of her Maker.

Within fifty years, Bertha's school, named the Margaret K. Long Girls' School (in honor of R. A. Long's mother), could boast of ten thousand students, a campus of three and one-half acres, a faculty of sixty teachers, a home economics building, a music department, a kindergarten, and plans for a primary school to complete a common school education based on the Bible.

The Margaret K. Long Girls' School had a reputation for its academic training as well as for turning out women of the highest character. They made it clear to all parents who wished to enroll their daughters that this was a Christian school. "If you do not want your daughter to become a Christian, do not enter her in this school," they informed parents. Several other women missionaries taught in the school at various times including Lavinia Oldham and Mary Rioch.

Bertha joined the ranks of a select few women in the Restoration Movement when she was ordained on August 14, 1904, by Archibald McLean at Angola, Indiana. She resigned as president of the girls' school in 1922 and spent two years doing evangelistic work in Osaka. She was then called back to do follow-up work among the alumnae of the school.

Her last furlough home in 1931 coincided with the decision of the Missionary Society to reduce its financial support of foreign missions. Bertha's heart ached as she realized that her return to Japan would not be funded. "I have been asked over and over again, this question, 'Do you wish to return to Japan?' What a question!" she responded. "I feel like screaming in reply, 'Do you want your family and your home? Do you want to breathe? Do you want to live?'"

She chastised her brotherhood with the statistics she had heard from others concerning the Disciples of Christ—"First in plea, Third in wealth, Fifth in membership, Twenty-fifth in giving." "Shame, shame on us who call ourselves disciples of Christ!" she lamented.

An Honored Visit

In 1935, on the occasion of the thirtieth anniversary of the founding of the school, the Japanese faculty, students, and friends sent an invitation to Bertha to come to Japan at their expense to celebrate the school's anniversary. She extended her visit to travel and live among them for two years, returning to the States for the last time in 1937.

During this last visit to Japan, the imperial government honored Bertha for her long service to Japanese women, giving her a certificate of appreciation bearing the Imperial Seal. She was among eight foreign heads of English-speaking schools invited by Princess Higashi-Fushimi to dine with her. All of those so honored had spent at least twenty-five years in institutional work among Japanese girls and women. The princess was interested in what they were doing for the education of women in Japan.

When Bertha arrived at the palace with the other guests, they were instructed in the proper etiquette for being introduced to the princess. "You will be presented to her one at a time as your names are called," they were told, "and as Miss Clawson has been in Japan the longest she will be presented first." When Bertha's name was called she walked toward the princess and was surprised that she came several steps toward Bertha, held out her hand and in perfect English said, "I am very glad to meet you, Miss Clawson. It was very kind of you to accept my invitation today."

After the presentations, they were ushered into a dining hall where Bertha sat opposite the princess and was asked to make an informal speech of appreciation on behalf of the Americans present. When the meal and afterdinner speeches were done, the guests engaged in personal conversation with the princess. Finally excusing herself, the princess left and her attendants showed the guests to the garden. As they prepared to leave, they signed their names in the guest book and were informed that strict etiquette required that each should call the following day to personally thank the hostess for her entertainment. Knowing that they were all busy women, however, the princess asked that they express their gratitude to her secretary as they left, absolving them from any further obligation to her.

Bertha recalled the luncheon as a rare opportunity that missionaries seldom enjoy. The certificate bearing the Imperial Seal remains a treasure in the archives of the Margaret K. Long Girls' School.

Bertha returned to the U.S. after this visit with the intention to work again in Japan, but the world situation prevented foreign travel. Instead, she made her home in California with another retired missionary, Jessie Asbury, and Jessie's sister Dr. Nina Stevens. Bertha continued to travel and speak on behalf of mission work until she broke her hip in 1947. When the fiftieth anniversary of the school approached in

1955, she made plans to attend; however, her hip injury prevented her from going. Instead, she sent the money she had saved for the trip to help build a primary school. Her nephew, field director of the Red Cross, was present at the anniversary ceremony and received a necklace from the Japanese on behalf of Bertha. Bertha died two years later on February 6, 1957, and is buried in Forest Lawn Cemetery in Los Angeles.

It was said of her that her middle name, Fidelia, was a "barometer to her life," a life "stamped over the world as her students have gone to the ends of the earth wearing in their hearts the image of Christ."

The Church of Christ missionaries were together for a photo in 1928. Back row (l-r): E. A. Rhodes, O. D. Bixler, J. M. McCaleb, Herman Fox, B. D. Morehead, Harry Robert Fox Sr. Middle row (l-r): Hettie Lee Ewing, Miss Fukazawa, Lillie Cypert, William Fox, Sarah Fox, Nellie Morehead, Clara Kennedy, Anna Bixler. Behind children: Pauline Fox.
Front row (l-r): Stanley Fox, Ramona Fox, Jane Bixler, Dorothy Bixler, Harry Robert Fox Jr., Logan Fox, Elizabeth Fox, Evelyn Fox, Martha Fox

Photo courtesy of Harry Robert Fox Jr.

CHAPTER NINE

CLARA KENNEDY: A CALL FOR MORE PRAYER

In July 1924, the *Word and Work*, a journal of the Churches of Christ, announced that Clara Kennedy of Maine, "who is commended by acquaintances and acceptable to Bro. McCaleb, expects to go to Japan to assist in the mission work this fall." Readers were advised where to send their contributions to fund her trip.

The next month, *Word and Work* announced that Clara was ready to embark for Japan but was in need of about four hundred dollars for her passage, equipment for work, and getting settled. The Portland, Maine, church was her sending congregation and she was to work under the direction of J. M. McCaleb in Tokyo. Charles M. Neal, the minister for the church in Dugger, Indiana, affirmed Clara's Christian character stating that he had baptized her in Portland in 1914 and believed her to be "fully efficient in the particular work which opens up for her in Japan. . . ."

FUNDED AND INFORMED

Apparently Clara received funds because the same issue of *Word and Work* confirmed she was on her way to the Island Empire as a missionary. The Portland Church was her main source of support but could only provide about half of the sixty dollars she needed monthly. In December of that year, it was reported that sixty-five dollars had been received for her support that month. The next month, January 1925, Clara received $62.50. Each month her sponsoring church in Portland sent her a check for sixty dollars carrying over any extra for the next month when contributions might run short. The surplus did not continue however, and subsequent issues of the journal included frequent appeals for more monthly support for Clara as well as other missionaries in various fields.

Sometimes it appears that Don Carlos Janes, who wrote the missionary column in *Word and Work* each month, would himself add the last few dollars needed. Janes was perhaps the foremost supporter of the independent missionaries throughout the world, financially and spiritually. His monthly column provided summaries of correspondence received from around the globe and strongly urged individuals and churches to do their part in providing for those on the field. In order to gain a better understanding of what the missionaries were experiencing, Janes and his wife made a worldwide tour from 1920 to 1922, staying in Japan eleven months. When they departed the Sunrise Kingdom in October 1921, missionary Lillie Cypert wrote: "Your coming to Japan and your short stay here has been a source of help and encouragement never to be forgotten. I have enjoyed it and been helped more even than you can know by your classes and many words of admonition and hope that the Lord helps me to pass it on to many other needy ones like myself."

Beginning in 1923 and continuing until his death in 1944, Janes not only wrote the missionary column in *Word and Work* but also published his own mission paper, *Booster's Bulletin.* After his death, the journal continued as *Missionary Messenger*, the same name of a four-page paper McCaleb produced in Japan each month from 1913 until 1919.

Keeping the churches at home informed and interested in their work was a major concern for missionaries. Several journals carried news and reports from those on the field, but individual supporters expected personal letters from those they funded. This could be a very time consuming task. Record-keeping also took up much of the workers' time, but it was imperative to maintain their integrity and account for every dollar (or penny) they received. This was especially true of the independent or direct-support workers in order to counter the accusation of the pro-society group that there was no accountability among those receiving funds directly.

EARLY YEARS

When Clara arrived in Japan, she spent her first two years assisting McCaleb in Zoshigaya and working with another single missionary, Lillie Cypert, in the dormitory of a girls' school that Lillie supervised. She taught English Bible classes at the Zoshigaya and Kamitomizaka churches in Tokyo and held singing classes at both places. "I spend much of my time working with the young people from the age of 12 to 18," she wrote home. Clara was noted for her vocal talent and was credited with having done much toward developing the singing within the churches in Japan.

Teaching the Japanese to sing was no easy task as Japanese music had no harmony. Everyone sang soprano. The missionaries spent many hours teaching their students how to sing in four-part harmony and considered it a success if they could master even two parts. Music was an open avenue to the hearts of people of all ages and once the door to the heart was opened, it was much easier to introduce the gospel message.

Clara adjusted to Japan fairly quickly, although she found it hard to stay warm in the winter months. She was grateful for a quilt someone had given her, explaining she put it on her bed "that very night for I needed it badly." Missionaries living in Japan relished bedding sent from home since native bedding was usually too short by at least a foot and the bed itself was only a pallet on the floor. At the head, a little bag of chaff about one foot by five inches was wrapped with a white towel to be used as a pillow.

Within a few months of Clara's arrival, she was given charge of the girls' dormitory. This was Clara's "baptism by fire" into the Japanese language as she was forced to speak in the native tongue to communicate with the girls. Four months later, Clara entered a language school to learn Japanese more thoroughly.

It was also during the spring of 1925, while Clara was in charge of the girls' dorm, that she sprained her ankle and was unable to walk for several days. She was also sick for about a month. Nevertheless, she carried on Bible classes, a singing class, and a women's class. After the Bible lesson, prayer, and singing, Clara included a lesson in foreign cooking. Once a week, she conducted a Bible class of twelve young men from a nearby university and taught several private Bible classes for individuals. Within four years, she had converted five people directly through her teaching. She reported that there were ten to twelve others whom she had a part in converting.

OPPOSITION TO MISSION WORK

The churches back in the States that supported the missionaries expected more results. Some felt there were enough "heathen" at home without going abroad to make converts. Others felt they had an obligation to teach their own countrymen before taking the gospel overseas. Some expressed disgust at the amount of money being spent in foreign fields with little results while the same money could produce many more baptisms through a Gospel Meeting at home. Other arguments were encountered when raising money and workers for the foreign field:

"It was the duty of the apostles to spread the gospel over the earth and they had no successors. Therefore we have no obligation to foreign missions."

"The gospel has been preached in all the world once and that is all the opportunity that should be given."

"Apostolic missionary work was accompanied by miracle-working power which we do not have: therefore, Christians are not now expected to do this work."

Articles from the missionaries in the brotherhood journals frequently attempted to counter these arguments. They contended that when the church knew more, they would do more, or that the more the church did in foreign fields, the more they would be willing to do at home. When the results seemed slow they reminded their supporters that it would require a great deal of time to turn people to Christ who had been brought up worshipping multiple gods. When they baptized someone, they wanted to be sure they understood the meaning of Jesus as a personal Savior, and God as the only true and living God. They had to convince the Japanese that Christianity is more than just one of the great religions of the world. They also had to deal with the false assurances of the Buddhist and Shinto priests who informed the people following the Russo-Japanese War that all those who had died in the war were now gods.

One approach was to work harder to produce greater results. This, however, could have the opposite effect as it took a toll on the missionaries' health, sometimes taking them out of operation for several months and causing added stress. Depending more on the Lord was a better response.

Clara and others urged those back home to pray earnestly for their work. "There is a need of constant prayer," she wrote in 1928. "I believe it the thing we need most of all in our work. Please pray for us all. Then you will be doing as great a part as we are in this, the Lord's business; moreover, I think we would see astonishing results in the work on the mission field."

FINANCIAL STRESS BUILDS

As if it weren't hard enough to maintain a consistent supply of financial support, when Clara was ready to come home to Maine on furlough in 1929, additional funds had to be solicited to pay her passage. When she was ready to return after two years at home (which she spent studying gospel music, child development, and Bible under R. H. Boll), she appealed once again for contributions for travel funds and asked for seventy-five dollars a month for support while in Japan. The funds were supplied, along with a letter of commendation from her home church in Portland, Maine, and she was back in Japan by December of 1931 working with the Zoshigaya church. Two months later she held three women's meetings with an attendance of twenty-five to thirty-five.

The Great Depression caused a reduction in the monthly contributions Clara and others received, thus causing additional stress. Clara was informed that one of her regular contributing churches would have to reduce their check from ten dollars to six dollars per month. "They were my best and most dependable supporters so it makes quite a difference," she wrote in March 1933. "But I'm sure the Lord will provide in some other way," she continued. "He hasn't failed me yet and I don't expect Him to now." Hinting that she might not be as optimistic as she sounded, she concluded with, "This world, in its present condition, isn't very pleasant and the joy of seeing our Lord will be wonderful. Please pray for us always."

Not to be discouraged for long, Clara struck out on her own in a new district in Japan in January 1934 where there was no church, no Sunday school, no kindergarten, no Christian work of any kind. "I don't know how I will come out financially," she wrote, "but I believe that God will supply my needs if the move is righteous in His sight, and I believe it is. Pray for me, brethren. I need it. . . . Even if because of the depression, you cannot give as you would like, you can help us to remove mountains through prayer."

She saw the fruit of her labors when one of her students, a fifteen-year-old girl, was baptized over the opposition of the girl's parents. "This means a lot in Japan," Clara explained. For an individual to become a Christian without first gaining the consent of her family would stamp her as disloyal and subject her to possible persecution. Even older women were not entirely free to make the choice for themselves.

Clara began a kindergarten in her new location and was soon responsible for domestic disturbances in her students' homes because the children refused to bow to the family idols saying it was silly and Jesus wouldn't be pleased. Little by little she went about sowing the seed and building relationships with the parents that would eventually lead to their conversion. While running this kindergarten, she began another Sunday school and Bible class an hour's train ride from Tokyo where a Christian brother lived who wanted her help to initiate evangelistic work in his neighborhood. He desired to have a Sunday school for his children and the opportunity to worship with other Christians.

This was more typical for Clara as she reported that she preferred to work with a church where there was a man to lead rather than trying to start a work by herself. The women on the mission field were very careful not to step outside the accepted role for their gender even when starting new churches. Even though most Churches of Christ would have disapproved of a woman teaching the Bible to men, it was permissible for them to do so in a foreign country. Those working under the Society sometimes mentioned "conducting services," "addressing a crowd," or "leading a church" when there were no males around to do so, but the majority of the women missionaries filled conventional roles as teachers of women and children—and occasionally men.

Clara concluded her work in Japan after twelve years, returning to the States in the winter of 1936. She made her home in Jefferson City, Missouri, for a while and then settled in St. Louis where she found secular employment. During World War II she worked with the 14th Street Church of Christ in Washington, D.C., and was instrumental in leading several young Japanese girls to the Lord when they were released from an internment camp.

CHAPTER TEN

ON THEIR OWN:
LESSER-KNOWN WOMEN WHO WENT INDEPENDENTLY

There were other single women who made contributions to the mission work in Japan. For various reasons, some only stayed for a short period of time. Discouragement accounted for some who stayed briefly. The insecurity of finances, loneliness, overwork, and a seeming lack of interest from those back home all mounted an attack on the most faithful workers at times.

Others were on the field for an extended term but very little is known about their work. The following women served in Japan independent from any missionary society. Some were initially sent by the Society but severed ties with the organization and continued their work as direct-support missionaries. Others went as independents trusting only in the promises of Christians back home to provide what they needed on the mission field.

NETTIE CRAYNON

Nettie Craynon of Kentucky arrived in 1896 although intending to go much earlier, in 1888. However, she became ill and was forced to wait until her health improved at which time Eugene Snodgrass assisted her in obtaining funding. Within a year of her arrival, she became dissatisfied with missionary work and entered secular employment in Tokyo as a typist. She maintained contact with the missionaries, however, and in March 1900 she attended the bedside of another missionary, Alice Bishop, as she lay dying. Nettie befriended the Bishops when they first arrived in the Island Empire in the fall of 1899 and reported having been especially impressed with Alice's selfless disposition. Nettie finally returned to the States in 1904 and married.

CHRISTINE PENROD

Christine Penrod worked with Loduska Wirick in Tokyo in 1897 to form a Bible chair for the first Church of Christ in the city. She was associated with the Florence Crittenden Home, which, along with the Salvation Army, formed the only rescue works of young women and girls in Japan. A board of interdenominational missionaries oversaw the mission and its purpose of preparing girls for domestic service or marriage or to support themselves by sewing.

The plight of young females from poor families in Japan was such that their families often chose to sell them in order to send the boys to school in England or the U.S. Christine made a fund-raising trip through the United States in 1913 seeking donations to build a hospital and reformatory adjacent to the Florence Crittenden Home. She explained that many Japanese families were "so poor that the daughters up to the age of 18, when they may be legally married, are a great burden." Christine knew of five girls who, after being sold, ran away and contemplated suicide.

She explained that her first work was to take care of girls who had run away so she could "save them morally, physically, and industrially." Even when touring in the States to raise funds, Christine was careful to make arrangements with other missionaries for the care of the young girls during her absence. Her work in Japan continued for thirty years. She was home again briefly in 1920, returning to Japan in December 1921 where she died the following year. She is buried in the Zoshigaya Reienn Foreign Cemetery in Japan.

CARRIE GOODRICH

Carrie Goodrich was a graduate of Hiram College in the class of 1896. The Euclid Avenue Christian Church in Cleveland, Ohio, supported her, sending her to Japan in September 1899. She sailed on board the same steamer as a medical missionary from the Cumberland Presbyterian Church, Dr. William D. Kelly. Less than a year later, Carrie resigned her work in Japan and married Dr. Kelly in Shanghai, China. Carrie relocated with him in China at a time when the nation was experiencing great unrest due to the Boxer Rebellion. She prophetically wrote in November 1901, "No other honor so appropriate could be given those who have sacrificed health and life for the salvation of China's millions, as to win all China from idols to the worship of the living God." One month later, on December 17, she died after a brief, five-day illness. One of her co-workers wrote, "She had endeared herself to us all by her consecrated life which we could not fail to observe. . . . Her whole heart was given to the work she hoped to do here among the women and children. She had unusually rare gifts in dealing with children and had great ambitions in the line of school work among them here." She was buried in Chengteh, China. Dr. Kelly later remarried and continued working in China after moving to the Reformed Presbyterian Church.

DR. GERTRUDE REMINGTON

Dr. Gertrude Remington served as a nurse in New York City and New Jersey for several years before graduating from the Southern School of Osteopathy in Franklin, Kentucky, where she received her medical license and attended church where James A. Harding preached. She had been raised in a Christian home and was the granddaughter of Christian Herman Dasher, the founder of the church in Valdosta, Georgia. Such a foundation had given her complete trust in the Lord to provide whatever she needed on the mission field. She wrote to J. M. McCaleb, "I am resting in God's care, and hoping He may prosper my way to Japan very soon if I can work for Him to His glory there. I shall be glad to come the first minute I see the way open."

When she finally had her travel funds in hand, she was asked if she needed any additional money before her departure. She replied, "No, I have plenty to take me to

Tokyo, and that is all I need now." Harding recommended her as one who was "well educated, of one of the best families, an earnest, gentle Christian, without being constrained to do so, she has devoted her life to ministering to the sick and dying."

The possibility of war between Russia and Japan was looming on the horizon at the time Gertrude sailed but she stated, "Should it arise, they might need me all the more; for there would be sick and wounded to care for, and broken bones to be bound up."

She left her home in Thomasville, Georgia, on January 26, 1904. She spent the next day in Nashville then traveled on to Bowling Green, Kentucky, to visit Potter Bible College (a school overseen by James A. Harding that closed in 1913). She reached San Francisco on February 8 to board the steamship *S.S. Gallic* on February 10. She reached Japan March 1, making her home temporarily with the McCalebs. As a hospitality gift, in back of their house Gertrude planted some pecan nuts she brought from Georgia. Thirty years later McCaleb was still enjoying the pecans from one of the trees that grew.

Gertrude immediately began practicing medicine, studying the language, and teaching Bible classes. She conducted a Bible class at the Kamitomizaka chapel on Sunday evenings from 6 to 7 P.M., after which McCaleb would preach. Unfortunately, she contracted tuberculosis, forcing her return to the States on October 17, 1906. The disease took her life the following year on November 24 in Pasadena, California.

ISABELLE WARD

Isabelle Ward went home to Wilmington, Illinois, to regain her health in October 1907. She had been in Japan for some time, but the exact date of her arrival is unknown. Her work centered around Hokkaido, the northern island of Japan. She spent the winter of 1907 in Colorado and Illinois. The following year, she visited the Cunninghams in New Haven, Pennsylvania, while they were on furlough, returning to her work in Japan in the fall of 1908. Isabelle's last trip home was in March 1919.

GRACE FARNHAM

Grace Farnham labored in Japan from 1925 to 1943. She served with Cunningham in the Yotsuya Mission until 1934 when she left his mission in protest over his methods. Grace continued her work independently from the Missionary Society, helping to establish the church in Mabashi.

When World War II broke out, Grace chose to remain in Tokyo to continue her Sunday school and kindergarten. She sent word of her well-being in the spring of 1942 through the Swiss legation in Tokyo to Switzerland, then from Switzerland to Cordell Hull in Washington, D.C., and from him to Grace's sister in Oregon, who forwarded her news to J. M. McCaleb in Los Angeles. Communications to Japan were also meager and Grace reported that for two years she received only one Red Cross letter and one cable.

"When war was declared," she said, "I felt rather lonely and far from home. But one of our dear Christian Japanese girls came almost every evening the first week to spend the night with me, because she thought I would feel lonely." Other Christian friends made an hour and a half trip every ten days during the winter of 1941 to bring her eggs.

When McCaleb left Japan the month before the attack on Pearl Harbor, he left nearly six thousand dollars in the care of Yunosuke Hiratsuka, one of the Japanese preachers he converted, with instructions to use the funds to provide for Grace as well as two other single women missionaries—Sarah Andrews and Lillie Cypert. McCaleb explained that Grace had been a close friend of his and the other two women. In the note she sent in 1942, she informed her sister that she was allowed to remain in her home and carry on her work as usual. Grace's news also raised the hopes of those worrying about Sarah and Lillie. McCaleb mistakenly drew the conclusion that since Grace was allowed to continue her work as usual and live in her home, the other two women would enjoy the same freedom and access to the funds he had left. This was not the case.

September 1942 Grace was interned in a school building and housed in one room with twelve other prisoners. Some had beds, she reported, and others slept on mats which they rolled up during the day. Food was furnished by a Tokyo restaurant but was scant and poorly cooked according to Grace. Occasionally they were able to get a little peanut butter or made a little jam after receiving some Red Cross supplies at Christmas consisting of sugar, dried fruit, and other staples. Every Sunday she met with four or five of her fellow missionaries to share communion.

Grace was among the Americans exchanged for Japanese civilians the following year. She was on board the *M.S. Gripsholm* that docked in New York on December 1, 1943, the same ship that brought Lillie Cypert home. It is not known if the two women knew the other was also on board since the ship was overcrowded including 670 missionaries from various religious groups. Grace returned to Japan after the war ended.

When foreigners wished to re-enter Japan in the post-war years, they had to bring their own supply of food since commodities were so depleted in the nation. Grace wrote to her supporters in 1947 that she was ready to sail on November 8 with one ton of food, consisting of flour, milk, sugar, meat, vegetables, canned and dried fruit, corn, and beans. She had also been given a projector, a set of dishes and silverware, and a few books to replace those lost during the war years. She still needed to replace her typewriter, phonograph, and records. Grace continued to serve in Japan until 1960 and passed away in Turner, Oregon, in 1984.

CECILE ELIZABETH HARDING

Cecile (sometimes written as Cecil) Elizabeth Harding was born in Kansas in 1885 but lived most of her life in the Pacific Northwest with her parents in eastern Washington State. By 1920, the family moved to Eugene, Oregon, probably in order to enroll their children at Eugene Bible University (renamed Northwest Christian College). Cecile sailed to Japan in 1925 in company with a fellow Oregonian, Grace Farnham. Cecile served in Japan only three years, working with the Temmabashi Christian Church. At the Baikwa Girls' School she taught English and music, both vocal and instrumental. Her service ended when she was compelled to return home to Spokane where she was diagnosed with cancer in 1928. She died within six months and is buried in the Garfield Cemetery in Whitman County, Washington.

When Grace Farnham returned to Japan following World War II, she took with her some slides and filmstrips purchased with a gift of one hundred dollars given to her by Cecile's parents in their daughter's memory. Grace intended to use them "to tell the gospel story," thus carrying on the work that Cecile had begun.

IRIS LYONS

Iris Lyons spent a year when she was twenty-three teaching twelve high school students in Cunningham's Yotsuya school from 1914 to 1915. Iris was from the First Christian Church of San Diego and was recommended by W. E. Crabtree. When she came back to her native country in 1915, she married George Lawrence Ritchie. Iris died in Palo Alto, California, in 1970.

EDITH LANKFORD

Edith Lankford from Hohenwald, Tennessee, spent a year in Japan arriving in December 1928. She traveled in company with B. D. Morehead and his wife. When she returned home in 1929, she was accompanied by Clara Kennedy. She had come to Japan by way of India where she visited other missionaries before reaching Japan. She passed away in 1949.

MAJEL LUSBY

Majel Lusby worked in Tokyo with Cunningham's Yotsuya Mission beginning in 1928. She came from Grayson, Kentucky, located in the northeast corner of the state. When Vivian Lemmon arrived in Tokyo in 1930, she made her home with Majel for the first few months. Majel ended her missionary work in 1931 and returned to Grayson where she married Ray Kelley in 1933. She died there in 1986.

RUTH SCHOONOVER

Ruth Schoonover was the first Christian Church missionary in the area of Tanabe, the third largest city in Wakayama Prefecture. She worked in other areas of Japan prior to moving to Tanabe, including teaching in the Yotsuya Mission in Tokyo in the early 1930s. She came to Tanabe in 1948 when she returned to Japan following World War II, but within six months her health failed and she died on the mission field. She was buried in the Mabashi Church of Christ cemetery in Tokyo. .

VIVIAN LEMMON

Four years after Ruth's death, another Christian missionary arrived in Tanabe to take Ruth's place. Vivian Lemmon was the daughter of pioneer evangelists in Washington State. She could recall sleeping in a crib beside the pulpit while her father preached and her mother led the singing in evangelistic meetings held in eastern Washington in the early 1900s. After high school and study at Ellison–White Conservatory of Music in Portland, Oregon, she attended Eugene Bible University. There she was introduced to Grace Farnham, who was home on her first furlough. Grace was at the college to make an appeal for another missionary to come help her in the Yotsuya Mission in Tokyo. She specifically wanted someone to assist with music and teach Bible classes. After a month of prayer and consultation, Vivian decided to answer Grace's plea and made preparations to join her in the Sunrise Kingdom. Vivian sailed on January 15, 1930.

She made her first home in Tokyo with Grace Farnham, Majel Lusby, and Ruth Schoonover and began teaching Bible classes in Cunningham's Yotsuya Mission. By 1934, the women had a falling out with Cunningham and resigned in protest. Vivian, Grace, and Ruth then began a new work in the Mabashi area of Tokyo. After her mother's death, Vivian opted to return to the States to care for her widowed father, arriving in Seattle in 1936. She would return to Japan in 1952 and take up the work in Tanabe that had been left vacant by Ruth Schoonover's death.

She invested more than twenty years in the work in Tanabe where the Kinan Church of Christ continued to be the only Church of Christ in Wakayama Prefecture. When past seventy years of age, Vivian believed her work on the mission field was nearly done. But then around 1976, she visited a young man in prison. Later, because his family rejected him and he knew little Japanese, he was paroled to Vivian. She moved to Osaka to make a home and find work for him. She also continued to teach piano at the Osaka Bible Seminary, lead English and Bible classes, and make a monthly trip to Tanabe to teach. By 1984, she was residing in Tanabe again where she died in 1987 at the age of eighty-five.

EMMA BEACH

Emma Beach left for Japan from Chattanooga, although she was born and reared in South Carolina. She served in Japan as a medical missionary beginning late in 1930.

She left Chattanooga on faith—she had not raised all of her support or travel funds. "I am planning on going just as though I had the entire amount, and the promise of full support after I reach the field," she confidently said. At that point she had eighty-five dollars in her travel fund and only fifteen dollars promised for monthly support. To make matters worse, she was robbed of all her money except nineteen cents on her way to the coast where her ship awaited. "Was robbed of every dollar I had but am going just the same," she exclaimed. "I surely need the Lord's hand to guide me now as I've never needed it before."

Emma was trained as a nurse and was able to assist missionaries O. D. and Anna Bixler with the birth of their child in Japan on March 26, 1931. She also taught Bible classes in the home of one of the young Japanese women, Tomie Yoshie. Two years later she wrote that she was in charge of a sanitarium for sick foreigners of all nations as well as the native Japanese. Being a nurse did not protect her from the diseases around her, and it was reported in the summer of 1932 that she and Clara Kennedy had both been sick. In addition to her nursing work she conducted Bible classes and English classes which developed "considerable interest" among the staff at the sanitarium. Her service in Japan concluded in 1934 when she returned to America arriving in Victoria, Canada, on the *S.S. Empress of Canada* July 18, 1934. She may have done additional work among the Japanese in Hawaii after that, as she was on the passenger manifest of the *S.S. Niagara* when it sailed from Honolulu to Victoria in 1937.

GRACE MADDEN

Grace Madden was a second-generation missionary, the daughter of veterans Milton and Maude Madden. Her parents had gone to Japan in 1895, sent by the Foreign Christian Missionary Society. In 1914, her father severed his ties to the Society because of their autocratic policies, especially concerning being moved from one location to another frequently and failing to support a policy of self-support among the Japanese churches. After a few years at home, he brought his family back to Japan to work independently in 1919. It was in the Tennoji church the following year that Grace was baptized into Christ on April 20. When Grace graduated from Bethany

College in 1931, she returned to Japan to take charge of the kindergarten in Osaka where the Maddens had purchased property to begin a Bible college for training preachers, the Osaka Bible Seminary. After marriage to Gerald Braley, a naval officer, Grace and her husband taught classes in the English night school. They left Japan prior to the start of World War II, but Grace found opportunity to use her knowledge of the language as an interpreter for the State Department and the Maryland Red Cross. She was a charter member of the Japanese flower arranging society, Ikebana International, and edited the magazine of the Sumi-e Society of America. She died in Sun City, Arizona, following bypass surgery in 1990.

EMILY CUNNINGHAM

Emily Cunningham, after being widowed by the sudden death of her husband, W. D. Cunningham, while on furlough in 1936, returned to Japan to take up the work alone in 1937. She remained until World War II forced her to leave. She was among the first Americans to be exchanged for Japanese civilians in June 1942 on the Swedish ship, the *M.S. Gripsholm*.

JENNIE MAY HIATT

Jennie May Hiatt was sent to Tokyo in September of 1908 to assist Fred and Myrtle Hagin. May, as she was known, was from Eureka, Illinois, where she received her A.B. degree from Eureka College. She continued her studies to receive the A.M. degree from the University of Wisconsin and then did graduate work at the University of Illinois. Her stay in Japan was of short duration as she was teaching school back in Illinois by 1910. She was a professor of French and German at Phillips University in Enid, Oklahoma, in 1937 and died in Illinois in 1969.

ALICE DRAPER

Around 1900, Alice Draper went to Japan. She is believed to be the daughter of a well-known physician in New York City, Dr. William H. Draper. This medical emphasis in her family drew Alice into volunteer work with the Red Cross near the end of the nineteenth century. Nothing is known of her service in Japan, but she returned home in 1907 and was married the following year to Edward Clark Carver, a graduate of Harvard class of 1900.

LEAN GILBERT

Lean Gilbert is listed as being an independent missionary in Japan for one year between 1923 and 1924. Nothing has been found concerning anyone by this name. However, there was a Lena Gilbert who arrived in Victoria, Canada, on May 26, 1924, on the *S.S. Empress of Asia* from Yokohama. This woman was an unmarried teacher living with her sisters in Vernon, Texas, in 1920. She married Jerry Briscoe on November 8, 1925 in Texas and died in Potter County, Texas, April 10, 1979.

ZORA HUFFMAN AND OLERA CRAIG

Earl West wrote in volume three of *The Search for the Ancient Order* that G. G. Taylor questioned the advisability of sending two women, Zora Huffman and Olera Craig of Colorado, to Japan. No record of Zora can be found. Olera was the daughter of William D. Craig who preached in Washington State in the 1890s. Olera was born around 1892 in Tennessee, but verification of her work in Japan is missing. Taylor's objections may have won out, preventing these women from going.

CHAPTER ELEVEN

THEY ALSO WENT FORTH: OTHERS SUPPORTED BY THE SOCIETIES

The Christian Woman's Board of Missions and the Foreign Christian Missionary Society operated separately for many years until they were both absorbed into the United Christian Missionary Society in 1920. The societies raised funds through donations and membership fees, the latter method objectionable to those opposed to the parachurch organizations. This did, however, provide a greater pool of finances to consistently support more workers on the field than the anti-society churches raised. The assurance of a regular paycheck, coupled with the emotional support provided by the parachurch organizations, may have encouraged more volunteers from the Christian Church and Disciples of Christ. Consequently, we find a larger number of missionaries, both married and single, male and female, who were sent by one of the societies than those who went out under the independent or direct-support movement.

The following women were supported by one of the missionary societies. Their sponsoring board determined where they would labor and frequently relocated them from one city to another when it was felt greater results could be obtained in a different location. Although they didn't have the same level of concern about finances as the independent missionaries, they faced the same struggles with the language, housing, weather, health issues, and opposition from the ancient traditions of the

Japanese religions. When the Great Depression struck worldwide in the 1930s, even the Society was forced to recall many of their foreign workers for lack of funds.

JESSIE ASBURY

Jessie Asbury determined to be a missionary when only fourteen years of age. Born near Germantown, Kentucky, her education was interrupted by a serious eye problem that was healed while visiting her sister, Dr. Nina Stevens, in 1896. Dr. Stevens was serving in Japan at the time with her husband under the Foreign Christian Missionary Society. In 1901, Jessie was appointed by the Society to work in Japan, also.

She conducted meetings and conferences for the Japanese women, did evangelistic work, and taught in a kindergarten. Through her efforts, a new kindergarten building was erected in Akita. While hosting a women's meeting she overheard one guest comment as she left, "That missionary kept talking about 'God, God.' I looked all around in the room and I could not see any god. Where was there a god in the house?" Fortunately it was a Christian woman to whom she made the remark, and it was explained that Christians do not keep their God on a shelf like Buddhists and Shintoists.

Jessie was credited with 50 percent of the converts in Osaka through her personal work. After retiring in 1932, she continued to work among the Japanese in Los Angeles, associating herself with the Vermont Street Christian Church. She began teaching the Japanese mothers the English language and American customs so they might better understand their children who were rapidly taking on Western ways. She died in Los Angeles in 1947.

EDITH WRIGHT

Edith Wright had a very short career in Japan, arriving in November 1902 and making her home with Bertha Clawson in Osaka. Her daily goal was "to help some poor soul." Upon her arrival, she wrote, "I am at my journey's end. I have had a royal welcome. There is no name for such hospitality in Indiana or Ohio. In a few days I shall begin my studies in earnest, with a prayer for health and strength and consecration and wisdom." Unfortunately her prayer was only partially granted, as she had to return to the United States the next year due to ill health. Apparently she found the climate of Europe more conducive to her health, as she made several trips abroad in later years, always returning to her home in Boston.

STELLA WALKER LEWIS

While a missionary candidate, Stella Walker Lewis met a young lawyer named Thomas A. Young. He was duly impressed with this young mission-minded woman, so much so that he decided to become a missionary also. Stella was sent to Japan in 1905 by the Foreign Christian Missionary Society, and Thomas began preparations for his career in missions with studies at Transylvania and the College of the Bible (now Lexington Theological Seminary) in Lexington, Kentucky. For the next six years, Stella worked in Osaka before coming home on her first furlough. While at home she and Thomas were married, and the two of them returned to Japan to work together in Fukishima. During her first term of service in Japan, she had worked among the women and children. Through cooking classes, in which the women were taught how to prepare nutritious food, and sewing classes, which gave them a means of earning money, the American missionary women developed relationships that opened the door for presenting the gospel. Stella and her husband continued to serve together in Japan until the outbreak of World War II, at which time they returned home to serve in local pastorates in Nebraska and Alabama.

MARY FRANCES LEDIARD

The first full-time missionary teacher employed in the Margaret K. Long Girls' School was Mary Frances Lediard. After thirteen years of service in the school, she was sent to Akita to assist in evangelistic work from 1919 to 1923. Mary was the daughter of a preacher in Ontario, Canada. Her mother was an early leader in the Ontario Woman's Missionary Society. Mary's sister Ella also became a missionary, serving in China. Mary received training to be a teacher at the Normal School in Toronto and taught for a year before going to Japan in 1906. In Japan she taught English, music, and Bible and at various times served as secretary, treasurer, and acting president of the Margaret K. Long Girls' School.

Between 1918 and 1923 she participated in an extensive evangelistic program in Akita and nearby towns. On one occasion, they had an international meeting with preaching from a Chinese pastor that was interpreted into Japanese. There were also people present from Great Britain as well as the United States. Mary marveled that people from four nations heard the gospel on one occasion, contemplating that the only way the world would be able to have unity was around the foot of the cross.

On another occasion, she was anticipating a day of rest and a picnic in a nearby town but ended up spending the day teaching other teachers at a school where one of her converts was employed. The three women and two men teachers who gathered to ask questions and study the Bible with her were very receptive to the gospel message. She was quick to make a disclaimer to her supporters in the States, however, that not everyone in the empire was waiting, Bible in hand, to be taught like these had been. But there were some who were anxious to hear and respond to the appeal of Christ. She was also responsible for the establishment of the Women's Christian Temperance Union in Akita.

She was in need of rest and change of scenery when she came home on furlough in 1921. She wrote to Laura Garst, "Any mattress will be a Seely[sic]; any chair an easy one; anything but green tea, nectar of the gods; and any food but rice and fish will be angel food to me." Despite the inconveniences of the Japanese culture and food, she loved Japan and spent over thirty years in the Sunrise Kingdom.

The Japanese were always ready for a celebration and frequently presented the missionaries with gifts on special occasions such as birthdays and even the anniversaries of their work in Japan. Mary received a lacquer cake box and tray from the church in Shinjo on the fifteenth anniversary of her work in the empire. Another type of celebration was enjoyed with a special Easter pageant Mary directed in Akita in 1922. It was quite an undertaking with scenery, costumes and a four-act play depicting the arrest, burial, and resurrection of Jesus plus a scene showing eleven types of Christian service. Over two hundred attended the show presented by her Sunday school children.

In 1923, Mary married fellow missionary Robert A. Doan. After a visit to her home in Owen Sound, Canada, they made a tour of mission points in China, India, and the Philippines, which broadened her interest in missions. "Although Japan is very dear to my heart," she told the crowd at an annual conference in 1925, "this wonderful experience has made my heart big enough to take in the whole world." Mary and her husband then made their home in Columbus, Ohio.

Following her husband's death in 1937 Mary returned to Japan for two more years, serving in the Margaret K. Long Girls' School and as hostess for the Kagawa Fellowship House.

When Mary was elected vice president of the United Christian Missionary Society in 1939, she returned to the United States to take her post. She retired in 1949 and passed away ten years later. At her memorial service she was praised for her "friendliness, graciousness, courage, devotion, and faith in the deeper dimensions of their meaning."

ROSE RUETTA JOHNSON

Rose Ruetta Johnson was the daughter of a Missouri Disciples' preacher, J. W. Johnson. She was educated at William Woods College, a junior college for women, and Missouri State Teacher's College before volunteering for mission work in Japan. In 1906, she was stationed in Akita for two years and then in Sendai for another two years before going to Fukushima. Her assignment was to teach English and Bible classes while also helping at the Christian Union Orphanage.

She returned home in June 1912 on the *Nippon Maru* to take care of her ailing mother, intending to return to Japan someday. In the meantime, Rose supported herself by selling encyclopedias. When she reached New Brighton, Pennsylvania, she checked into a ladies' boarding house and asked where the local Disciples of Christ met. The landlady immediately ran to the gentlemen's boarding house and told the landlady there, "I've found a lady for your Mr. Calderwood!" Jesse Calderwood was also the son of a Disciples' preacher. Rose became Mrs. Jesse S. Calderwood in 1918. The couple made their home in New Brighton, where she continued to serve the Christian Churches of Beaver Valley until her death in 1957.

EDITH PARKER

Following graduation from the University of Missouri with a B.S. degree in education, Edith Parker taught in the public schools for five years, the State Normal school, and the University of Missouri, then joined the faculty of William Woods College. Edith went to Japan in November 1909. She relinquished a very desirable position at the college and went to the mission field on one-third of the salary.

Even in Japan she was a loyal Missourian. She was a charter member of the Japan Alumni Association of the University of Missouri and served as the vice president of the club when it formed in 1920. The Alumni Association's first meeting was held at the Seiyo-ken Café in Tokyo where they met to learn the outcome of the Missouri–Kansas football game played just two days before.

She taught in the Margaret K. Long Girls' School in Tokyo, opening the department of Home Economics that became a model for the Japanese government. She was known for her deep devotion to the Japanese people, "a remarkable will power and tenacity, and a great capacity for friendship."

When she returned from a furlough in 1920, she arrived with a typewriter, a gift that became a valuable asset to their work. Unfortunately her service in Japan ended when she contracted smallpox upon returning from a vacation in China. She and her friend Mary Lediard had gone to China to spend Christmas with friends and see the work of the China Mission. As they sailed back to Japan, she complained of not feeling well but dismissed it as only seasickness. By the time they reached Kobe, she was so weak that it seemed best to go directly to the International Hospital. She died in the isolation unit on January 13, 1923. She had supervised the construction of several new buildings for the Margaret K. Long Girls' School including a new chapel that was filled with students, alumnae, and friends who came to attend her memorial service.

The head of the school read Scripture, led in prayer, and paid tribute to "Parkie." He spoke of her devotion and sacrifice for the school and education. Others spoke also, and the choir sang "In the Secret of His Presence." Many expressions of sorrow and appreciation were given and other musical offerings were made. In her homeland, a memorial service was held February 18 with her father, three sisters, and three brothers present. Her supporting church in Carrollton, Missouri, also held a memorial service later that month.

"It is only by knowing what she would expect of me," her closest friend Mary Lediard wrote, "that I feel I can keep on. She was full of life and energy and a great hope and I will not disappoint her by weakness now." She gave her life for Japan, crowding into fourteen years a lifetime of service for her adopted country.

GRETCHEN GARST

The first Restoration missionaries on Japanese soil, Charles and Laura Garst in 1883, reared their own female missionary with the birth of Gretchen in Akita on April 1, 1887. When older, Gretchen served in Japan under the direction of the Missionary Society from 1912 to 1925. She had received her kindergarten teaching certificate from Drake University before departing for Japan where she worked in the kindergarten of Akita, her birthplace.

Kindergarten work was one of the most common outreach methods implemented by the missionaries. In a country where homes, yards, and streets were small and crowded, a large, pleasant room and more than the usual yard space for children to play drew an overwhelming response. Some kindergartens featured a mothers' room where the women could wait for the children they had come to retrieve. It included a library of helpful books on the care of children and the Christian message. A small charcoal fire in the hibachi was usually kept burning to warm the room and heat the traditional kettle of hot water for tea. The conversations held here between teachers and mothers brought about the formation of the Mothers' Clubs where more formal instruction occurred.

As the kindergarten children were taught about Jesus and the Bible, they readily took the new information back to their homes where their parents learned from them. Gretchen told about a little boy of six named Taro who was heard mumbling in his bed after his mother had tucked him in for the night. Looking in at him, she found him sitting up on his little sleeping mat saying something to himself. She told him to lie down and go to sleep. He lay back down but she heard him mumbling quietly again. When she came back into the room he said to her, "You do not know what I was doing, do you? Well, I was praying to the real God. I always do, every morning and every night. I learned it at kindergarten. Mother, why don't you and father pray to the real God, too? He loves everybody, especially little children." He then proceeded to teach her the song he had learned in kindergarten— "Waga Shu Yesu," ("Jesus Loves Me").

Gretchen spent her first furlough in 1918 studying at Columbia University in New York, then resumed her work in Japan where her kindergarten students celebrated her tenth anniversary in their country with a special program. The mothers, children, and graduates joined in the celebration with speeches and songs. Two high school pupils representing the graduates made speeches of appreciation. The governor of the province came in person and spoke in appreciation of the kindergarten and her work in it. The city sent a representative as did the parents' club and the church. Each one spoke in high terms of the school and especially the better understanding that had resulted between the Japanese and the foreigners. They said the missionaries had an international influence as many who saw them judged all foreigners by their example. "It thus becomes our privilege," Gretchen wrote, "to hold up to them the very highest ideals of our country."

Gretchen helped prepare for the opening of a kindergarten in Fukushima in 1923. When she returned to the United States, she worked with the welfare departments in Des Moines and Chicago. Further studies at Drake resulted in a B.S.E. degree in 1928. She retired from her welfare work in 1935 because of ill health and died from cancer on April 25, 1952.

WINIFRED BROWN

Winifred Brown taught music for one term in Margaret K. Long Girls' School in 1913. She was from Bonham, Texas, where she graduated from Carlton College. During the remainder of her five years in Japan, she was in charge of the Takinogawa kindergarten. After returning home in 1918, she resumed teaching music in San Angelo, Texas, until she was married to William Powell Lee in 1920. The newlyweds took up residence in Arizona where she did freelance writing.

After being widowed in 1939, Winifred became the assistant superintendent of the Juliette Fowler Home for children in Dallas, followed by a position as secretary to the superintendent of the Texas School for the Blind in Austin. She had been employed as a music teacher at the School for the Blind before going to Japan.

ADA SCOTT

Ada Scott served with the Disciples of Christ in Tokyo from 1916 to 1925. She was a granddaughter of Norman Dunshee, a pioneer educator at Hiram College and first faculty member of Drake University. Ada graduated from Drake University with her B.E. and B.S. degrees and gained teaching experience in the elementary schools at Kelly and Nevada, Iowa, and in the high school at Granger, Iowa.

In Tokyo, she taught kindergarten and Bible classes in the Margaret K. Long Girls' School and continued the work begun by Mary Rioch. While teaching at the Mary Rioch School, she had the opportunity of rescuing a young Japanese girl who was about to be sold by her brothers to pay off a debt. Ada paid the money the family needed and undertook responsibility for seeing that the girl was given an education and proper training.

Ada supervised kindergartens, taught English and Bible, and visited in the Japanese homes. She was in Karuizawa when the big earthquake of 1923 occurred. For several days afterward, she reported that she and nearly everyone else went to bed partially dressed ready to leave the house at a moment's notice in case of another quake. They were placed under martial law and women were forbidden to enter the city. By God's grace, none of the Restoration missionaries were injured or killed and none of the church buildings destroyed, although Ada had to conduct classes in the school gym afterward because the school building was condemned as unsafe. She requested thirty-five thousand dollars from the Society to make the needed repairs.

Ada came back to the States in February 1925 due to the illness of her father and never returned to Japan. Following her service in Japan she taught in the high school at Chariton, Iowa, for twenty years until her death in October 1946.

JEWEL PALMER

When the big earthquake struck Tokyo in 1923, Jewel Palmer was home on furlough where she was completing her master's degree at Columbia University in New York. Her undergraduate degrees were from the University of Missouri and Christian College of Columbia, Missouri. From 1918 to 1921 she was assigned to teach English in the Christy Institute at Osaka.

The Christy Institute was founded by the Disciples of Christ Mission in Japan in 1914. It was named in honor of William Christy whose widow donated the funds for the building although R. A. Long donated the land where it stood. The school offered night classes for men and women in English, writing, typewriting, and shorthand. It also included an evening chapel service and Sunday Bible classes. By its tenth anniversary, enrollment reached four hundred boys and two hundred girls.

Jewel was popular with her students due to her sense of humor and understanding heart. Upon her return from furlough in 1925, she was made head of the home economics department of the Margaret K. Long Girls' School. She also conducted a Bible class for girls from a nearby government school. The government authorities were opposed to this effort and discouraged the girls from attending. However, the young women continued to come and when they returned to their homes in outlying areas, they took the Christian message with them.

When Jewel's mother became seriously ill, she returned to Missouri to care for her, arriving in San Francisco on January 5, 1929, on the *Siberia Maru*. Back home, she became the director of young people's missionary organizations in Missouri. From 1933 to 1939 she worked as a resident secretary for the YWCA in Pittsburgh then went to Enid, Oklahoma, to be the chairwoman of the home economics department of Phillips University. During World War II, she was granted a leave of absence to teach home economics in the high school at the Jerome War Relocation Center, a Japanese internment camp in Arkansas. The government requested her services since Jewel was one of few Americans who could speak and write Japanese. She died in 1949 in Enid.

EDITH HAGIN

A second-generation missionary, Edith Hagin spent her first tour of service in Japan as a child of missionaries Fred and Myrtle Hagin. She was educated in the school for American children in Tokyo, and at the age of thirteen came to the United States accompanied by Jessie Asbury who was leaving on furlough. Edith was back in Tokyo two years later in 1908 when she was hospitalized with tuberculosis. Her mother brought her Stateside early the next year when her health improved sufficiently for travel. Fully recovered, she graduated from the Los Angeles State Normal School and, after teaching in California for a time, enlisted as a missionary for Japan in 1919.

Her early years in Japan served her well as she was able to complete two years of study at the language school in just seven months.

She was in Tokyo during the earthquake of 1923 and witnessed firsthand the devastation and destruction of the city. She wrote of being in the train station when the quake struck and, due to the aftershocks, was unable to continue to her destination of Tabata, north of Tokyo. "There were fires all around, though not so very near, and the sun shone dimly and blood-red through the smoke," she recalled. "Ashes and red-hot bits of paper fell from the smoke which the high wind carried over our heads."

She spent one night sleeping outside with fellow missionaries since they were unsure if their school buildings and homes were safe. The fires continued to spread the day after the quake and came nearer their buildings. When they were about to evacuate they changed their minds and instead started inviting other refugees into the school building for shelter. They housed nearly a thousand that night. The next day they were instructed to return to Karuizawa. Edith's luggage with all her clothing was burned in the Tokyo train station, leaving her with a cape that she used as a blanket and cover-all.

She was informed that many people lost their lives as they stood on the pier in Yokohama when the pier sank. One report claimed that only two houses were left standing in Yokohama.

The following year, Edith returned to the States, and in 1928 she married John D. Francis. He passed away in 1949, and she was later married to Anthony Rumfalo. Her own death occurred in 1968, and she is buried beside her first husband in Rose Hills, California.

HELEN RICHEY

Helen Richey graduated from Ohio Wesleyan University in 1913 and did graduate work at Florida State College for Women. After a brief teaching career she entered the College of Missions at Indianapolis in 1919 to prepare for service in Japan. The College of Missions was opened by Indianapolis Christians in 1910 to prepare young people for mission work. Arriving in Japan in 1921, she was involved in evangelism and teaching in the Government Normal School for Girls at Fukishima. She shared living quarters with Gretchen Garst as well as a local female evangelist and a Japanese helper, Kei Fujimori. Miss Fujimori was the niece of Otoshige Fujimori, who operated one of the most successful Christian missions in the Sunrise Kingdom.

Taking advantage of the loss of government textbooks that were burned in the 1923 earthquake, Helen and her co-workers began offering English classes for the children after regular school hours and invited them to their home where they could build deeper relationships. As a result, some of the girls began coming to the girls' Bible class on Sunday and the Christian Endeavor Society meetings on Tuesday afternoons.

Helen told about a burglary at another missionary's home in 1924. K. C. Hendricks' home was broken into. The thief made off with Hendricks' watch and English New Testament. Within a few days the Japanese thief was apprehended and jailed. Hendricks went to the jail and presented the burglar with a Japanese Bible that the inmate would be able to read in his own language.

When Helen returned from furlough in 1926, she joined the faculty at Margaret K. Long Girls' School. At the time of her next furlough in 1932, she traveled home on the *Tatsuta Maru* in company with Rose Armbruster. Funding was being withdrawn from foreign missions due to the Depression and they both were forced to remain in the States.

Helen went to Florida where she taught in Leon High School in Tallahassee and then at Pikeville College for Women. She earned her M.A. from Pikeville College in 1936. As one who enjoyed learning as well as teaching, she did research at Florida State College for Women (now Florida State University) and took classes at Columbia University, Iowa State College, and the University of Tennessee.

In Florida she was active in the Capital Christian Church in Tallahassee participating in the church school, the choir, the women's council and the businesswomen's guild.

AMY JEAN ROBISON

As Amy Jean Robison departed for Japan in 1921 after graduating from the College of Missions, she stated, "It is with joy and enthusiasm that I turn my steps toward Japan to help those people be true lovers." Love must have been on her mind because after four years in Japan as a single missionary she married a fellow mission-ary, Hubert C. Sarvis, in March 1924. Before and after her marriage, she taught in the Christy Institute, donating her services without pay following her marriage. She and her husband suffered a grievous loss when their newborn son died shortly after they returned from furlough in 1926. Failing health ended her husband's labors when he died in September 1931, but Amy Jean continued her work among the Tennoji Chris-tian Church until 1935.

On September 21, 1934, a tidal wave swept over Osaka where widow Amy Jean and her daughters lived and worked. Winds up to 125 miles per hour pushed waves that overwhelmed two-story buildings in the city of three and one-half million people. On Sotojima, an island in the bay where a leper colony resided, people climbed trees or telegraph poles to escape the water, but the wind beat them off like autumn leaves into the water below. When the waters receded, they found 260 bodies in the mud and sand. In the city, nearly 900 homes were washed away while 200,000 other homes were damaged. For a week they were without electricity, gas, or running water. Transporta-tion came to a halt, and no phone or telegraph service was available. Amy Jean and her children were not hurt, though their house was damaged. The death toll from the storm was nearly 1,700 with 1,600 of those being school children.

The next year, Amy Jean returned to the States and taught English in the high school in Oskaloosa, Iowa. She married again in 1970 to Ira Dorwin Crewdson, also a widowed missionary. He died five years later and Amy Jean passed away in 1987.

BERTHA DOUGLAS

After graduating from the Eugene Bible University in Oregon, Bertha Douglas took an additional year of study at the College of Missions before going to Japan in 1920. With five years of prior experience teaching in the public schools in Fresno, she was put in charge of the Kizukawa and Tennoji kindergartens in Osaka. These schools represented two distinct types of families in Japan. One was composed of children from industrial homes and the other with children from prosperous middle class families.

Despite health struggles, Bertha also assisted at the Christy Institute in Osaka before illness forced her to resign, arriving in San Francisco on June 13, 1925. For the next four years she worked among the Japanese in San Bernardino and then retired to Santa Cruz.

LOIS LEHMAN

Lois Lehman worked under the Foreign Christian Missionary Society from 1922 to 1927. A graduate of Hiram College and Northwestern University, she had a special aptitude for music, art, and kindergarten work. Due to the Tokyo earthquake of 1923, her studies at the Language Institute were cut short, and she was sent to Akita to teach in the kindergarten. Following the earthquake, she led her kindergarten students in a benevolent campaign to provide kimonos for the destitute children of Tokyo and Yokohama.

In preparation for the visit of the Crown Prince of Japan to Akita, Lois taught her students to influence their parents to abandon drinking saki during the celebration. She introduced the children to grape juice and stressed the fact that the prince abstained from strong drink, thus making their parents' drinking displeasing to the prince. She also included a lesson on the detrimental effects of alcohol on a person's body.

When the Society reorganized the work in Japan, they decided there was no longer a need for a kindergarten teacher since the local citizens were able to handle the teaching responsibilities. Lois was relieved of her position and resigned from the Society in 1928. The Society issued a statement that "Miss Lehman has rendered excellent service and her resignation is accepted with deep regret."

After two more years of study, she returned to Japan under the United Church of Canada as the foreign director of their Kindergarten Training School in Tokyo. Upon completion of her work there, she made her home in Indiana and Wisconsin.

JESSIE M. TROUT

Jessie M. Trout, a Canadian, was appointed by the Society to serve in Japan in 1921. Mary Lediard Doan, another Canadian whom she had known in Ontario, inspired her to make missionary work her career. Jessie's work in Japan was centered in Akita where she worked with women and children in the kindergarten and the Margaret K. Long Girls' School. Along with Lois Lehman, she took over the work of Gretchen Garst when Gretchen moved from Akita to Fukushima in the fall of 1924.

She returned home in 1933 to work in Society headquarters when missionary funding was reduced. At the time the Society missionaries were recalled, their work force in Japan shrank from a high of thirty-two to only four. Jessie was able to join those in the field again in 1935 under the direction of the United Christian Missionary Society. After five years, Jessie's mother became ill and died in 1940, which brought Jessie back to Canada shortly before the outbreak of World War II. Due to the mounting international tensions, she did not return to Japan as planned in 1941.

While home during the war, she wrote *Forward in Missions and Education* and for two years was the national secretary of *World Call*, a journal of the Missionary Society churches. In 1946, she was selected to serve as executive secretary of the Society. Butler University honored her in 1955 with the D.D. degree and Bethany College conferred on her the L.L.D. degree. She is best remembered as the founder of the Christian Women's Fellowship, a women's auxiliary group. Desiring to end her career as it had begun, she resigned from the national staff of the Society in 1961 and went on special assignment as a field liaison, visiting missions in India, Nepal, Paraguay, Argentina, Congo, the Philippines, Hong Kong, Taiwan, Japan, and Okinawa. She passed away at her home in Ontario, Canada in 1990.

CLARA CROSNO

A very brief term of service was seen by Clara Crosno, a graduate of Phillips University at Enid, Oklahoma. She also completed a year of preparation at the College of Missions where her classmates included Amy Jean Robison and Jessie Trout. All three were sent to Japan in September 1921. However, the effect of the climate on Clara's health forced her to resign in July of the next year. Her love for the Japanese people continued, and she found a field of work among the Japanese population in Rocky Ford, Colorado. In 1932, she became Mrs. Joseph Ahlstrom and made her home in Cheyenne, Wyoming, where she died in 1977.

HAZEL HARKER

Ill health also forced the early return of Hazel Harker. Trained as a musician at Butler University, she entered the mission field in 1923 as an instructor of music at the Margaret K. Long Girls' School. She worked with the Tennoji Church at Osaka before spending eight weeks in the International Hospital in Tokyo as a patient. There she learned a great deal about the truly "international" aspect of the institution. In the room next to her was a German woman and across the hall were a French mother and new baby. Down the hallway was a little Russian girl, and a little further on was the daughter of the English Bishop. There were two other U.S. patients and many Japanese as well. Two of the interns were Filipinos.

The cause of her hospitalization was unexplained, but it involved surgery performed by a Japanese doctor. Shortly after her operation, she returned to the States, arriving in Los Angeles November 4, 1925, on the *S.S. President Taft*. While in Los Angeles, she worked with the Japanese at the Japanese Christian Institute, organizing club activities for children and the mothers' clubs and speaking to various groups about her short stay in Japan.

She was a prolific writer, supplying Sunday school lessons and programs on a regular basis in the pages of *World Call*. Hazel moved to the Midwest in 1929 to serve as assistant pastor of the Jackson Boulevard Church in Chicago. From there, she went to Indianapolis to work in the Marion County welfare department among the aged and blind. In 1936, she served as the Director of Religious Education for the church in Lebanon, Indiana. She died in Indiana in 1963.

MARTHA ELLIS GIBSON

Martha Ellis Gibson received an A.A. degree from William Woods College in 1919 and the B.A. degree from Washington University, St. Louis, in 1921. She was engaged in social service work for a year for the Board of Education of St. Louis before enrolling in the College of Missions. Upon completion of her studies, she was sent to Japan to work among the women. She was scheduled to sail from San Francisco on August 15, 1924, on the *Siberia Maru*. Her departure was delayed, however, and she traveled in company with Jewel Palmer in January 1925 as Jewel returned from a furlough. Stationed in Fukushima, Martha taught in the Sunday school, visited Japanese women in their homes and assisted in cooking classes. When the couple she was working with, Mr. and Mrs. K. C. Hendricks, went on furlough, Martha had full charge of the work in Fukushima and handled all the finances of the mission as their treasurer.

Her furlough in 1929 was spent in India where she visited her twin sister, Harriet, who was serving in that mission field with her husband, Carl Vissering. Martha also took classes at the University of Chicago before returning to Japan in 1930. She was recalled to the United States in 1932 as the Society reduced their mission efforts and was given governance of the sales literature department of the United Christian Missionary Society.

Desiring to be on the mission field again, she was sent to Asuncion, Paraguay, in 1938 where she was the head of the dormitory for the boarding school girls at Colegio Internacional. Once again, her next furlough was spent in other mission work as she worked at White Swan, Washington, in 1943 among the Yakima Indian Christian Mission as matron for the girls' dorm. In 1947, she was elected secretary of the

Christian Women's Missionary Council of Missouri and worked for the Red Cross in St. Louis, her hometown.

Doris Cunningham

Doris Cunningham was born in Japan in 1902, the daughter of missionaries W. D. and Emily Cunningham. After formal education in the U.S., she returned to the land of her birth to work under the United Christian Missionary Society beginning in 1927.

Arriving shortly after the death of Emperor Yoshihito that occurred on Christmas Day 1926, Doris was thrust into the Japanese customs surrounding the emperor's funeral. The entire country went into a period of mourning for six days when there was to be no music or rejoicing of any kind. Some of the Christian churches held Sunday services as usual but without any singing while others sang a cappella. Foreigners, including Doris, scarcely smiled for fear of doing something offensive. Flags were draped with black crepe, and many men wore black armbands for the full fifty days until the funeral.

This early glimpse of government rituals prepared Doris for the role she would play later as the wife of an American Consul General following World War II. Doris ended her work in Japan in 1929 to return to the United States where she was married the following year to Leo Sturgeon who had worked for the State Department in China since 1925. In 1946 he was sent to Tokyo where Doris and their children joined him. There is no evidence she ever left the land of her birth again.

Virginia Dee Yoho

Virginia Dee Yoho's father was an early Christian preacher. Her mother, Elva Alma (Wayman) Yoho, died shortly after Dee's birth and is buried in "God's Acre" on Alexander Campbell's Bethany farm. Dee, as she was known, graduated from Bethany College then worked for the United Christian Missionary Society in their religious education department beginning in 1926. During the spring of 1928, she took a four-month leave of absence to do graduate work at Yale University. In 1930, The United Christian Missionary Society sent her to Japan.

She had just completed language school when the Society had to reduce their expenses and recalled their missionaries from Japan. However, she chose to remain on the field and took a position with St. Luke's Hospital in Tokyo. Deciding to become a nurse, she entered Yale University Hospital in September 1933. By the time she graduated in 1936, the world situation precluded her return to Japan.

She was employed by the New Haven Hospital where she became head nurse and later a supervisor before becoming an instructor of nursing administration at Yale University School of Nursing. Joining the Army Nurse Corp in the first year after the attack on Pearl Harbor, she was sent to New Zealand where she was appointed chief medical nurse and assistant to the chief nurse of the 39th General Hospital, a two thousand-bed unit in Auckland. In 1944, she was transferred to Saipan where she remained until September 1945. The following January, she was discharged with the rank of major.

A week after her discharge, she was married to Lt. Col. Allan Eldridge and they both enrolled at the School of Agriculture at the University of Arkansas. From there, they went to Storrs, Connecticut, to work on the administrative staff of the University of Connecticut. She was active in community events as president of the Storrs Women's Club and the American Association of University Women. She died in Indianapolis in 1976.

EDITH SHIMMEL AND ETHEL JONES

Edith Shimmel and Ethel Jones were both graduates of Cincinnati Bible Seminary and had been schoolteachers before going to Japan in 1934. Edith was a graduate of Grimal College in New York, the Lock Haven (Pa.) Normal School, and Pierce School of Business Administration in Philadelphia. She was sent to Japan by First Church of Christ in Philipsburg, Pennsylvania.

Ethel was from Granville, Ohio, where she graduated from Denison University. She was about thirty years younger than Edith but they became close friends. In 1939, they decided to move their work to Hawaii and then to the Philippines where they were both interned as prisoners during World War II. Johnson Bible College in Knoxville, Tennessee, honored Edith with an endowment in her name.

CHAPTER TWELVE

SARAH ANDREWS: A ONE-WAY TICKET

A s mentioned previously, Kate V. Johnson had a tremendous influence on her young pupil/friend, Adele Shepherd. Adele's daughter Sarah Andrews was twelve years old when Kate visited Adele's family during her 1904 furlough. Like her mother, Sarah was captivated by the stories Kate told about the people in the Land of the Rising Sun.

Two years later, at the age of fourteen, Sarah was baptized by I. B. Bradley, the minister for the Walnut Street Church of Christ, which her parents had helped to start in Dickson, Tennessee. She told Bradley shortly after her baptism that she hoped to go to Japan as a missionary someday "to help teach them about the true God and the Savior; and I am going to work for that and try to prepare myself for the work."

Sarah's early desire to go to Japan was confirmed when veteran missionary J. M. McCaleb paid a visit to the Walnut Street Church while he was home on furlough in 1909. McCaleb's home was in Middle Tennessee and he visited several churches in and around Nashville while in the States before returning to Japan in 1912. After young Sarah heard him speak concerning the need for gospel workers in Japan, she told him she planned to go to Japan as a missionary when she graduated from school. McCaleb responded, "Let me know when you are ready to come."

In 1913, she wrote to McCaleb, "You remember a few years ago when you were at Dickson that a little girl came to you after the last lecture and told you she was going to be a missionary in Japan. I am now 21 years old and am making preparation to fulfill this, my greatest desire." McCaleb published this letter in his *Missionary Messenger* paper in February of 1915.

McCaleb commented that he was pleased to know that she had "held sacred" her vow and still desired to enter the mission field. He recalled that there were other young people who had made a similar statement to him when he had been in the States and wondered if any of them would also follow through.

On March 28, 1915, Sarah wrote again, "I am ready for you to announce in the papers that I wish to go to Japan in the fall." She affirmed that she intended to work within the bounds of the New Testament by teaching women and children. Her announcement appeared in *Word and Work* in August of that year along with her picture. "Miss Sarah Andrews, of Dickson, Tenn., who expects to join the workers in Japan this fall. Funds for her passage are asked for, and contributions may be sent to I. B. Bradley, Dickson, Tenn. Funds for passage of Bro. J. M. McCaleb's new son-in-law, John T. Glenn and wife, who will accompany Sister Andrews may be sent to D. C. Janes, or R. H. Boll, Louisville, Ky., or to W. W. Freeman, Cordell, Okla." As it turned out, McCaleb's daughter and husband did not go to Japan as announced, and Sarah sailed alone.

McCaleb wrote again in June of having been in correspondence with "a sister at Dickson, Tenn., in reference to her coming to Japan as a missionary, a matter she has had her heart set on for several years. The sister is Miss Sarah Andrews." She had taken a physical exam by a doctor in Dickson who affirmed that Sarah was "a strong, healthy girl in every respect." One might question this conclusion in light of several health problems Sarah experienced on the mission field.

This announcement was followed by a letter from I. B. Bradley to McCaleb offering assurance that Bradley would be responsible to help her raise her support and forward funds to her once she got to Japan. Bradley endorsed Sarah, pledged to have a talk with her parents concerning her going, and even said he would try to get the Walnut Street Church to assume most if not all of her support. Bradley

Sarah Andrews

Photo courtesy of Bettie Lundy

may have been overly optimistic about the ability of the Walnut Street Church. As shown in Sarah's regular financial reports, she received funds from individuals and churches from several states, but the Walnut Street Church was never listed specifically as a contributor. Most likely the fifty dollars that I. B. Bradley regularly sent to her which was broken down as from "various sources," included monies from the church in Dickson. Some of the members sent support directly to her and at least one of the Sunday school classes collected money for her that Winifred Shelton sent to Sarah regularly.

"She is dependable and will make an earnest, zealous worker," Bradley assured McCaleb. "I baptized her and have watched her development and noted with delight her zeal and earnestness, as well as her loyalty to the Lord's revealed will and way. . . . You must take good care of her while we loan her to you and the Japan work," Bradley concluded.

EARLY PREPARATION

Three months later, Sarah had only raised one third of her necessary funds. Bradley's appeals continued on her behalf. "She is full of zeal and energy for the work," he said, "and is equipped with good literary training. She has been a student of God's Word since her childhood and has great reverence for the revealed way of the Lord."

Indeed, her upbringing in the Andrews' home had prepared her well for service in the kingdom of God. When Sarah's parents, Will and Adele Andrews, moved from Hurricane Mills to Dickson in 1888, they found a handful who shared their faith but no meeting place. Dickson was a railroad town but there was no congregation of the Church of Christ. Adele was determined to establish a group of New Testament Christians in their new hometown.

With the assistance of an elderly widow, Rachel Haynes, Adele and Will arranged to use a room above the Dickson Bank and Trust Company on Main Street where the small church of thirteen members could meet. Andrews paid the rent for the first five months until others could share the cost. A protracted Gospel Meeting with J. W. Grant was held in May 1891 that resulted in the organization of the first Church of Christ in Dickson. Two years later, they built a house of worship on the corner of Walnut Street and Center Avenue where it still stands today although much enlarged.

In addition to the religious education Sarah received at the Walnut Street Church, she acquired an outstanding academic foundation as well. In September 1891, the year before Sarah's birth, the Dickson Normal College opened. The school had such an outstanding reputation that people sent their children there from great distances. After completing her primary education in the Dickson public schools, Sarah enrolled at the Dickson Normal College, but before she could complete her studies there, the State Normal School opened in Memphis and the Dickson school was closed. Sarah transferred to the school in Memphis to finish her training in classical and practical courses. She became adept at public speaking, art, first aid, home economics, and kindergarten instruction.

In July 1915, the *Gospel Advocate* carried another appeal from Sarah's minister for Christians to send funds to enable Sarah to go to Japan as an assistant to the missionaries already there. "She has never been urged to go," Bradley wrote, "but from a little girl she has cherished this idea and desire and has grown up with this as the supreme purpose of her life . . . the question now is, will the churches of Christ send her and stand by her?"

Bradley assured the *Advocate* readers that she was "loyal to God and his will, believing in the simplicity of the apostolic times, and is opposed to all innovations in the church and the work of the Lord. She is opposed to women preaching in the public assembly of the saints and is a modest, quiet, Christian woman, full of zeal and piety. She has a good knowledge of the word of God and is a constant student of the Bible."

The goal was to raise three hundred dollars for her travel and first month's support by the middle of September so that she could sail with John T. Glenn and his wife (the daughter and son-in-law of J. M. McCaleb). Bradley had even calculated that if each of the "loyal churches" (anti-missionary society churches) would send just five cents, it would provide enough for her ocean passage and several months' expenses. He had already received sixty-six dollars.

The *Advocate* carried a second, more forceful request from Bradley in September. "Brethren and sisters, we have advocated that mission work be done by the church as God's missionary institution and the independent missionary. Shall we 'fall down' now and let the work fall because of a lack of support? There is scarcely one-third enough funds on hand now for the expenses of her trip to the Orient, and the call has been before the readers of the *Gospel Advocate* about three months. We feel there has not been enough consideration and prayer given this question by the churches. . . . This is the King's business, and it requires haste. . . . The demand is urgent; only about four or five weeks remain now to get the funds ready for the trip. Shall she be forced to forego the start for Japan because the church is too close to supply the means?"

He went on to lecture his readers about the obligation they had to send the gospel to those still in darkness, then he concluded with a final appeal. "Miss Andrews is worthy and one of the most consecrated young women in the church of Christ, we believe. Send me your contribution for this work at once. Do not put it off, you might overlook it later; do it now, and let's have enough in hand and to spare when the time comes for her departure. She expects to start during the month of October. Remember, 'now is the accepted time—to-day.'" The same appeal appeared in the November issue of McCaleb's *Missionary Messenger*.

Bradley then gave an accounting of all the funds that had thus far been received for Sarah's work along with the name of each contributor and the amount they had given. The total was eighty-six dollars.

October came and went without Sarah sailing. The appeal for financial support continued in *Word and Work* in December. "Bro. and Sister Glenn, with Sister Sarah Andrews of Dickson, Tenn., are ready and waiting to enter the work in Tokyo, Japan. Who will aid in sending them out?"

Finally, Sarah's father provided her with the remaining funds to purchase a one-way ticket on a steamer for Japan. She left her family behind in Dickson on Christmas Day 1915 to travel to Vancouver, British Columbia, by train. The January 1916 *Word and Work* reported, "Miss Sarah Andrews passed through Louisville recently on her way to Japan for missionary work. We were exceedingly well impressed with her spirit and her pluck, her culture, and her forceful personality. She is making the trip unaccompanied."

In Vancouver, she boarded the *S.S. Empress of Japan* to cross the ocean. She had just celebrated her twenty-third birthday.

JOURNEY TO JAPAN

Her first letter back home appeared in McCaleb's *Missionary Messenger* in February 1916. "Through the goodness, mercy, and protecting care of the Great Ruler of the Universe the steamship *Empress of Japan,* landed at Yokohama, January 16, 1916. On account of a continuous head wind, together with two very bad storms, she was more than 24 hours late. However I am indeed thankful, yea beyond expression for the successful voyage to the land of the Rising Sun, a land filled with wonder and mystery for me."

Word and Work published portions of a letter from her in March. "Sister Sarah Andrews writes from Tokyo: 'I am happy to tell you I am safe in Japan. Had a very successful as well as a pleasant trip. . . . Sent Bro. McCaleb a wireless on Thursday before landing on Sunday, January 16, and he made all arrangements before I arrived.'"

Her long letter published in *Missionary Messenger* included a description of her train trip from Chicago to Vancouver, British Columbia, and how awed she was at the scenery she had never imagined—the broad prairies, the Canadian Rockies, snow-drifts up to twenty-three feet, and British soldiers guarding bridges from possible attack by the Germans. The train ride had taken her from Kentucky to Vancouver in seven days arriving at 10 A.M. on January 1. She had three hours until her ship would weigh anchor.

She occupied a stateroom with another missionary also headed for Japan whom she did not name. She described her as a veteran of eleven years, but it may not have been a missionary from the Restoration churches, as other denominations had missionaries on the field also.

This first of many ocean voyages Sarah would experience was very rough with only two days exception. She described being in a frightening storm at sea but drew comfort from the solution found in Psalm 107: "They are at their wits end. Then they cry unto Jehovah." Hinting at the severity of the storm or perhaps her own fear of it, she related that "God was very near and dear unto me through the entire trip."

She was also missing her family and friends back home but said she was comforted by the words of a poem:

> There is a scene where spirits blend
> Where friend holds fellowship with friend
> Though sunder'd far, by faith we meet,
> Around the common mercy-seat.

When Sarah arrived in Japan, there were already eight churches meeting regularly to worship and commune together and nine Sunday schools with five hundred children enrolled. In places where there were not enough Christians to organize a church, "preaching stations" were designated instead. The male missionaries took turns visiting these stations to preach as their schedules allowed.

The intense humidity in Tokyo during the summers was almost unbearable for foreigners. "The doors swell so they won't shut; paint becomes soft and sticky; matches won't strike; shoes mould and turn green; grain sprouts in the patch; fruits and vegetables rot; trees become top-heavy and bend over; growing corn turns pale; envelopes stick and all the house becomes musty and damp," McCaleb described. "It is necessary to build a fire at intervals to dry things out."

Many of the missionaries sought relief by renting a cottage in the mountains, including Sarah, who was already showing signs of stress. In fact, by May, just four months after her arrival in Japan, doctors had advised her to leave the country due to a "severe nervous affliction." McCaleb rented a house in Karuizawa, and the Christian missionaries in Tokyo took refuge there from the heat.

Riding the train from Tokyo to Karuizawa involved a journey through grain fields before reaching the base of the mountains where an electric train replaced the steam engine and proceeded to push the train upwards. They traversed a series of twenty-six tunnels so closely spaced that the train could be in two or three at the same time.

Upon reaching the station, the missionaries continued through the business district of the village for a mile or two to the resort. McCaleb's house was situated on the edge of the resort surrounded by evergreens and native trees. Inside was an unpainted post with pencil marks and the familiar names of missionaries as well as the McCaleb children who were then in school in Tennessee.

Although away from the city, Sarah's work did not stop. She received a letter from one of her students expressing interest in studying with her. "If you teach me my questions I will be glad. I hope to be versed in the commands of God by your kindness," the girl wrote. "After I understand the outline of the New Testament I will

Sarah Andrews in Japan
Photo courtesy of Bettie Lundy

be a faithful believer, and hope to exert my best for religion. Please give me the light of knowledge and let me joy in the brightness when you return to Tokyo."

The summer respite wasn't sufficient to bolster Sarah's constitution however, and in October *Word and Work* reported that Sarah "had some nervous trouble. She is a very ambitious missionary." Evidently she was under a great deal of stress. Trying to learn the language was the major burden and paying the tuition at the language school compounded it. An appeal was made for additional contributions toward her support to help with this extra financial obligation.

More Fund-Raising

W. D. Hockaday, who had met Sarah when she traveled through Louisville on her way to Japan, wrote an inspiring letter to the *Missionary Messenger* in which he connected Sarah's willingness to go to a foreign land with the necessity of Christians to put the Word into practice. Upon bidding Sarah farewell when she left Louisville, he wrote, "She started to Japan alone. Have I the faith to do that? Have you? What if she were my sister or yours? Where would our hearts be? If this were the case with either of us, would that dollar be locked in an unbreakable vault in which selfish interest alone is the combination?"

He continued urging his readers to support Sarah financially. "Why may I not get the congregation where I live to send monthly to Sister Andrews' support? . . . When JESUS said, 'Go ye therefore and teach all nations,' did he mean Sister Andrews more than he did you? . . . She is starting to her great work wrapped in the blood-stained banner of King Jesus, and all the powers of Satan cannot stop her unless the Lord in his infinite wisdom thinks best for her to stop. . . . Brother and Sister, the Lord is trusting us as messengers through whom he may supply their need. Shall he wait in vain for us to respond?"

In June, Sarah reported that she had received a total of $174.80 during the first six months on the field—an average of less than $30 a month. The following month she reported having received $57.50 but added that she had also received several letters of encouragement, "all of which were greatly appreciated. Knowing that brothers and sisters in the Lord are praying for me in this great work, makes me more courageous to press on." By autumn, the situation had not improved. Bradley reported having been able to send $50 only five times in eight months which put Sarah $150 short of what she needed.

McCaleb added an explanation. "$50 a month is a modest sum, and when it falls even much below this she must suffer lack." He also mentioned that she would need more than that in order to pay $65 for the language school where she would study Japanese. "Being very economical in her manner of life she has been able to keep even with her financial obligations up to the present," McCaleb wrote. "But she is preparing to enter the Japanese language school for missionaries in a few days without her first instalment [*sic*] for tuition—$40. I hope churches or individuals may be induced to give regularly toward her support and work till she is adequately supported."

He commended her saying, "Sister Sarah never complains, but is contented with such things as she has—and without what she doesn't have. For this very reason she is all the more worthy of a more generous support. I am taking the liberty to write this not letting her know it, for I have an idea she would object."

Once her language school had begun, McCaleb continued to appeal to churches to send $5.50 a month to defray the tuition expenses. He even suggested they could make it an even six dollars since she had to pay five cents a day for carfare, which amounted to about one dollar a month more. "In coming to Japan to make Christ known to this people Sister Sarah has done what few are willing to do and that many could not do if they were willing; but here is something you *can* do and have part with her in the great work she has undertaken," he urged. "Get together; decide; begin NOW!"

At the end of her first year, in December 1916, I. B. Bradley reported being able to send fifty dollars to Sarah the previous month from contributions that had come through him. He was hoping to have that much to send near the end of December but said, "remittances have not been regular."

HER FIRST CONVERTS

Despite the difficulty of learning the language and fretting about finances, Sarah was responsible for the baptism of ten women in her first year on the field. One of those young converts was O'Iki Naemura. (In Old Japan a woman's name, if not more than two syllables, was prefixed by O. The suffix *san* is honorific and dropped in familiar conversation.) Iki san remained with Sarah as her helper and friend for the duration of Sarah's life. Her first year also included adjusting to the "many curious smells" she found in Tokyo and attending two funerals—the first for a young mother of six children and the second for the woman's newborn baby who died two weeks later. A Buddhist priest conducted the mother's funeral while McCaleb conducted the infant's funeral, in which he offered consolation and admonition for the living. The Buddhist funeral ritual was addressed to the dead for the consolation of the departed spirit.

The Buddhist priest, with a shaved head, wore a garment of white cotton, the traditional color for funerals. The Japanese wear black for weddings. He wailed and chanted as he occasionally rubbed a string of beads between his hands. The plain, unadorned coffin was lowered into a small grave as family and friends tossed in clods of dirt. Bodies were sometimes buried in a sitting position in order to save space. More often they were cremated. A small post was set in one corner of the grave and the dirt tramped down. A little incense was burned and the relatives dispersed without weeping, as it was customary to repress emotion.

The Christian funeral service two weeks later offered an obvious contrast between the two religions. McCaleb's sermon was filled with comfort and hope provided in the resurrection. It was a clear demonstration of the need for more messengers who could bring the hope found in Jesus Christ to a nation of fifty million people dying without hope.

There was also a wedding to celebrate as two young Japanese Christians were united in marriage by McCaleb. Tomie Yoshie had been converted when she lived in the McCalebs' home one summer while attending Japan Women's University in Tokyo. She was wed to Kojiro Sato, the native evangelist in Zoshigaya. They continued to be faithful workers in the church throughout their lives.

The Japanese were becoming much more receptive of the gospel message and when a meeting was held in Kobe the missionaries had to ask the Christians to stay away in order to make room for more than two thousand non-Christians who

Sarah Andrews and her helper O'Iki Naemura

Photo courtesy of Bettie Lundy

crowded into the building. The need for more workers in the field was obvious and every issue of *Word and Work* and *Missionary Messenger* carried appeals for others who would be willing to go abroad with the Good News. Few were willing to make the sacrifice and many even discouraged their children from entering mission work. McCaleb wrote about meeting parents in many churches where he spoke while on furlough who requested he not put it into the heads of their sons and daughters to leave home for foreign work.

Recruiting workers for Japan was particularly difficult. C. C. Klingman and his wife had spent a little over three years in Japan when they were forced to return to the States when Mrs. Klingman's health failed in 1912. She died of tuberculosis four years later and Klingman blamed their years in Japan for her death. He publicly stated that he could never return to Japan and did not have the heart to encourage anyone else to go. McCaleb conceded that there were some who should not be encouraged to work in Japan. "Japan goes hard with some people," he said. "It is perilous to life, involves much expense, discourages the churches and is a great disappointment to those who attempt it." But he reasoned, "Missionaries are not the only people who get sick and die."

CHAPTER THIRTEEN

LILLIE CYPERT: A CO-WORKER FOR SARAH

In November 1916, nearly a year after Sarah Andrews' arrival, a glimmer of hope appeared as J. M. McCaleb reported that a schoolmistress in Arkansas had volunteered to go to Japan. "Miss Lillie Cypert, now engaged in teaching in Arkansas, writes in a letter Sept. 11 as follows: 'I think I have my mind thoroughly made up concerning my work, and would be glad for you to make mention of it in the paper at any time.'" McCaleb went on to state that she was in perfect health, "a very important item for one thinking of coming as a missionary to Japan."

He asked, "What church will make her its missionary and, either of itself or in cooperation with other churches, will send this new worker to the field?" McCaleb suggested that the Henderson church where Lillie had attended while studying at Freed–Hardeman College (now University) should take the lead in asking other West Tennessee churches to aid in supporting her. The goal was fifty dollars a month, which McCaleb was certain could easily be raised by the "goodly number" of churches in West Tennessee and "the burden would be so light they wouldn't even feel it."

Word and Work carried the announcement in August the following year: "Sister Lillie Cypert, of Marshall, Ark., has signified her willingness to go to Japan as soon as funds are ready. She has stood a fine physical examination and Bro. McCaleb approves her purpose."

At the same time that McCaleb was announcing Lillie's decision and need for funding, this note also appeared: "Bro. McCaleb reports that 'Miss Andrews came through her operation (for appendicitis) beautifully! . . . Sisters Andrews and Miss [Alice] Miller have been to the mountains awhile.'" Recuperating from an appendectomy in the middle of the summer in Tokyo would have been more than sufficient cause for Sarah to escape the city heat for a mountain retreat. The following month, readers were reassured that "Sister Andrews is getting along much better since her operation for appendicitis."

Meanwhile Lillie Cypert continued to make preparations for her departure to join in the work in Japan. Don Carlos Janes wrote in his column in *Word and Work*, "Her physician's statement of her condition is very favorable, and those who wish her to go to the field at the earliest possible date may send their assistance to me. . . . I think it would be fine for her to be associated with Sister Andrews and the others in Tokyo." In September, he reported contributions for her support "have come in nicely." With the assistance of O. E. Billingsley, Lillie's fund-raising was quite successful as Janes wrote two months later, "Our newest missionary, Sister Lillie Cypert, arrived in Japan on October 25."

Lillie Delenzia Cypert was born in Oak Flat, Arkansas, on May 27, 1890. Her father Eli died when she was only four, and her mother Euphamia ("Famie") remarried five years later to James Franklin Dyer. Six children from this second marriage brought the total to ten children in the Cypert–Dyer household.

Educated at Freed–Hardeman College in Henderson, Tennessee, she began teaching school in Searcy County, Arkansas. It is not known what inspired Lillie to choose Japan as a mission field or to make missionary work the pursuit of her life. It may have been an emphasis placed on missions and Japan in particular while she was at Freed–Hardemann. Or it may have come from having read about the famous British missionary-explorer in Africa, Dr. David Livingston, when she was a young girl and determined to do something like that with her own life.

Whatever prompted her, she sailed from Vancouver, British Columbia, on October 5, 1917, and arrived in Yokohama twenty days later. Sarah Andrews was pleased

Lillie Cypert
Photo courtesy of Steve Yanai

to have a co-worker, and they became good friends. Lillie wrote, "I am so grateful to have Miss Andrews here. I don't see how I could get along without her."

Finances continued to be a struggle for Lillie and all of the independent missionaries. Just seven months into her work, *Word and Work* reported that Lillie's support had fallen short about fifty dollars during the first three months of 1918, which meant she was living on less than forty dollars per month. In September, Janes noted that funds coming for Lillie in July had only amounted to $32.25, far below her budget of sixty dollars per month. Later that year, she wrote a personal note about her finances that was published in the journal. "Of course I feel very happy when the check is large enough to meet my needs until I will not have to depend on some one else to pay my bills," she wrote.

J. M. McCaleb had made some wise investments in property in Japan and lived very frugally. As a result he was sometimes able to assist those such as Lillie and Sarah when their support fell short. In the same issue of *Word and Work* in which Lillie wrote the above note, McCaleb wrote, "Your good letter with check for $49 gratefully received. I am turning it all over to Miss Cypert as she is short and I can get on." The total funds she received during her first year in Japan amounted to $661.99.

Still Lillie trusted in the generosity of individuals and churches to provide what she needed. "I am not at all afraid to trust it to the Lord to put it into the hearts of His people to supply my needs if I am faithful to Him," she wrote to Don Carlos Janes. "I appreciate your efforts and the great interest you have taken in my support more than I can tell, but please don't worry about it. If it is little, I shall be happy and thankful just the same, and shall remember Matt. 6:33 and Rom. 8:26."

Lillie may have had more reason to be concerned about her support than others as her sponsoring congregation changed several times. Her initial forwarding agent had been Nellie Straiton of Fort Worth, Texas. When Nellie switched to a Christian Church, Lillie's support was taken over by the Brownwood, Texas, church. In 1931 this church was forced to discontinue the work due to the Depression, and Lillie's support was taken over by the Southside Church of Christ in Fort Worth until 1936. It then shifted to Gladewater, Texas, which continued to send her funds until she returned during World War II.

As with other missionaries, learning the language became her first priority. Even before mastering how to communicate, she assisted Sarah and McCaleb in their work by handing out tracts to the thousands who assembled in the parks on feast days or walked to the temples. She taught English to those who wanted eagerly to learn the western language and she visited the physically and spiritually sick.

Sarah Launches out on Her Own

In the fall of 1919, Sarah felt comfortable enough with the language and decided to move out on her own to begin a new work. Most of her fellow missionaries had concentrated their efforts in the capital city of Tokyo leaving the outlying cities in the country with no knowledge of Christ. She wrote letters to the mayors of several of these towns and made visits to a few. She then chose Okitsu, a city on Suruga Bay, about one hundred miles southwest of Tokyo. She and Iki san set up housekeeping in the town of about 8,600 where the gospel had never penetrated before.

Her method of evangelism was to open a kindergarten and teach the children the way of the cross. This would open doors of opportunity for her into the children's homes where she could teach the mothers and eventually the fathers. When officials asked Sarah not to include prayer or Christian songs in her kindergarten, she refused. Her response only brought greater interest as she had nearly eighty-five applications for admission, thirty-two of whom she accepted for enrollment.

"One of the larger children wept," Sarah said, "when she heard the story of Joseph for the first time." She also reported that the work in Okitsu had grown much larger than she had expected and would need more workers and more finances. Indeed, her next communication reported 150 children receiving instruction. She went to double sessions, one in the morning for the younger children and a second one in the afternoon for the older children. The afternoon session had to move one class out of doors if it was not raining because they had outgrown the building.

Within the first four months, she had three converts. Before the end of 1920, Sarah sent word of nine baptisms, including a young girl she was helping through school, Iki san's sixty-one-year-old mother, the assistant stationmaster's son, an ex-naval officer, an ex-subchief of a village, a sixteen-year-old boy, a seventy-year-old Presbyterian man, and two others.

When there were baptisms to be performed, Sarah could send for one of the local Japanese preachers. Hirosuke Ishiguro had been converted in 1910 by Bert Hon, a Restoration missionary who only spent one year in Japan. But in 1920, Ishiguro was preparing to sail to the U.S., leaving his wife and baby behind, while he enrolled at Abilene Christian College to receive more formal training in Bible and evangelism. After graduating from ACC, he decided to stay in the country and sent for his family to join him. They settled in Los Angeles where he began the first Japanese Church of Christ in America, known as the Westside Church of Christ.

With Ishiguro no longer available to baptize Sarah's converts, she sent for Otoshige Fujimori. He had to ride a train ten hours to get to Sarah's village, but he readily complied.

"Oto," as he was affectionately known, had been converted while living in Michigan when he was twenty-three. In Detroit, he had been taken under the wing of a German immigrant, Frederick Wagner, who became like a father to Fujimori and matured him in the faith. After studying with Wagner for eighteen months, Otoshige Fujimori was baptized by W. D. Campbell on May 13, 1894, at the Plum Street Church of Christ in Detroit.

One of Fujimori's brothers was a Shinto priest, and Fujimori had a deep desire to take the gospel to his family and countrymen. At Fujimori's insistence, the sixty-two-year-old Wagner accompanied him to Japan in 1898 where they bought fifty acres of land for $1,200—funds provided by the Plum Street Church and one of its elders, John Gray. Following Alexander Campbell's idea of a "Christian colony" where the Christian life and doctrine would serve as evangelism tools, they began to reach the surrounding neighbors with Christianity. On this farm, "in the backwoods of Shimousa," seven miles from Sawara, Fujimori opened a school, ran a self-supporting farm, orphan home, home for the elderly, a church, and served six preaching stations. Although he had eight children of his own, he also adopted two orphans and five of his brother's children after his brother died. The colony eventually planted four other daughter churches at Sawara, Omigawa, Takahagi, and Ushibori. Responsible for three hundred to four hundred baptisms, it was one of the most successful outreach efforts of any of the Restoration missionaries.

Fujimori came again to Sarah's town in the summer of 1920 to conduct street preaching. One of their converts, Mr. Murata, worked in a sandal factory. His father tried to burn the Bible Sarah had given him when he was baptized.

In addition to teaching in her kindergarten, each week Sarah taught three Bible classes and an English class in her home. Another hour each week was spent teaching in the local high school. In-between classes she distributed tracts and Bible portions from house to house. She was blessed to have Miss Kaji, a girl she had converted in Tokyo, come to Okitsu to aid in the work.

THE NEED FOR SUITABLE HOUSING

With Sarah's move from Tokyo, Lillie and a few other missionaries were left to share McCaleb's house as he had gone Stateside on furlough in January of that year. Before his departure Lillie and Sarah had gone to his cabin on the steamship and placed some flowers by his mirror. Back at the house, Lillie planted a garden in the yard and grew cabbage, tomatoes, corn, beans, beets, lettuce, onions, spinach, cucumbers, squash, watermelon, muskmelon, peanuts, carrots, parsnips, okra, and a few Japanese vegetables in addition to flowers. Picking strawberries, making jam, sewing, cooking, and cleaning occupied much of her time.

McCaleb's Western-style house was comfortable, but suitable housing was another obstacle for the missionaries. Japanese-style homes were too cold in the winter and too hot in the summer with their paper walls. During one summer there were seventeen missionaries taking refuge from the heat in McCaleb's summerhouse at Karuizawa. This number included eleven adults, three infants, two Japanese women, and a little girl. This count did not even include Lillie who had taken up temporary residence in a nearby hotel.

McCaleb made an appeal for funds to build Western-style homes for the missionaries. "The needs of the work in Japan include at least two houses for missionary residences," he wrote. "These need to be sanitary structures built like our homes are built and will cost with the ground about $10,000 in all." He assured the churches back home that these houses would be held as church property. Don Carlos Janes endorsed the campaign, and he wrote, "We should not endanger a missionary's health in a Japanese house, especially when it can so easily be avoided." McCaleb added, "To live in Japanese houses is inconvenient, trying on the health, and expensive."

It was claimed that the average life of a Western man in Japan was three and one-half years, even less for a woman. Many broke down and had to leave the country within six months. Nervousness, tuberculosis, and rheumatism were the principal enemies to a person's health. The summer retreat to Karuizawa during the "steamy season" of July and August offered the missionaries a chance to enjoy a season of study, recreation, and fellowship with other missionaries in addition to rebuilding their health.

McCaleb had a Western-style house built of wood in Tokyo in 1907 that still stands today as a state owned cultural monument. A celebration was held there in November 2007 to commemorate the 100th anniversary of the house. McCaleb's iron bed was borrowed from Japanese preacher Motoyuki Nomura and placed on display in McCaleb's former bedroom while Alice Miller's organ provided music for the occasion.

McCaleb's School

For five years, McCaleb conducted a boys' training school in a rented house, enrolling about thirty per term. With the completion of his house, there was room for the students as well as space where McCaleb could live with the boys. Unlike other boarding schools in Japan that were notorious for immorality, McCaleb's school enforced strict rules. The young men would attend regular classes provided by the government in the daytime and receive Bible lessons at the boarding school each evening. Tuition and donations allowed the school to be self-supporting. Lillie and Sarah had both been put to work teaching in the school when they first arrived in Tokyo even though girls were not allowed to board there and only a few females ever attended classes.

Mr. Iida, one of the students from McCaleb's first class of 1907, approached McCaleb with the idea of beginning a school for girls where they could be taught sewing and other domestic skills in addition to the Bible. McCaleb mortgaged the boys' school building, expecting that tuition and donations for the girls' school would pay off the mortgage and eventually the second school would become self-supporting also. A house was purchased for the girls' school that opened December 2, 1918, with twenty-two girls enrolled. Lillie was the matron of the dormitory and taught English and Bible. The enrollment grew to seventy the next year. This new position, along with teaching in the Zoshigaya kindergarten and Bible school and adult Bible classes, filled her days. On Friday evenings she hosted a Bible class for workers and teachers. Sunday mornings, a prayer meeting was held in her home at 6 A.M.

The boys' school had its problems, including an uprising by the students in response to some of McCaleb's policies, but it continued to house, educate, and influence young men for twenty years. The girls' school, however, closed by 1920 due to a disagreement between Lillie and Iida, who had become the principal. Lillie discovered that Iida was smoking cigarettes and then lied about it to McCaleb. She would not tolerate such behavior and resigned in protest. Without her participation, the school declined and had to close. McCaleb also learned that Iida favored sprinkling for baptism and probably would have terminated him anyway.

Overall, the work was going well in 1920. Since the arrival of the Azbill group in 1892 there had been over a thousand people converted and ten congregations established. There were three hundred children in Sunday schools in addition to three charity schools, a school for young men, and another for young women. Three native Japanese preachers reported good results. Sarah's work at Okitsu was growing, and she could report another three baptisms by June. Lillie continued her work at the Zoshigaya Children's Bible School. Alice Miller, although advancing in age, was said to be "as fervent as can be" and expected to stay on the field "until she is called home or the Lord returns." Two married couples, the Rhodes and Bixlers, were actively engaged in language study, working among the existing churches and filling in until McCaleb returned from furlough. Another couple, the Herman Foxes,

Back row: J.M. McCaleb, Lillie Cypert holding infant, O.D. Bixler, Anna Bixler, E.A. Rhodes, Bess Rhodes holding child, Harry Robert Fox holding infant, Pauline Fox, Sarah Fox, Herman Fox, Irene Janes, Don Carlos Janes.
Tokyo 1921
Photo courtesy of Steve Yanai

arrived mid-year, joining Herman's twin brother Harry Robert and his family who had arrived six months earlier.

Most conversions by missionaries were the result of teaching English Bible classes or Sunday schools. Two evenings a week, Sarah conducted a Bible class for eighteen grammar school boys who had come to her asking to be taught about Christ. Other times, converts came from chance meetings. O. D. Bixler told about meeting a man while walking along the beach at Okitsu one morning. Recognizing Bixler as an American, the Japanese man spoke to him in English. The conversation turned to Bixler's business as a minister. He told the man about Sarah Andrews' work there in Okitsu and encouraged him to contact her for Bible study. Not long after, Bixler received word from Sarah that Tsunenori Aoki, who had been referred to her by Bixler, was engaged in serious and earnest study with her. It wasn't long before Bixler was asked to baptize him.

"We went to the quiet waters on the shore of Okitsu bay about eleven o'clock in the evening," Bixler wrote, "and in the presence of others whom he had already taught almost unto full surrender, he was baptized." Five more soon followed as this new convert continued to share his changed life.

On the evening of his baptism, Aoki spoke to a group of young men in Sarah's English class, telling them of his "past mistakes and hatred for Christianity." As a military commander, he had even ordered his men to give their Bibles to him and, in their presence, tore them up and threw them into the sea. The evening after his baptism, Aoki preached on the street to the people in his town. About two hundred stood around to listen and stayed until the end of his sermon. It was his desire to preach the gospel full time among his people.

Still the road was uphill and strewn with disappointments as Sarah tried to overcome the generations of superstition and tradition. When the town chief of her village died, his wife threw herself under a train in accordance with the Japanese custom of committing suicide after a husband's death.

CHAPTER FOURTEEN

FURLOUGHS TO RECRUIT AND RECOUP

Early in 1921, Sarah Andrews took her first furlough home, leaving Japan January 7. J. M. McCaleb, along with Don Carlos Janes and his wife, who were in Japan for a visit, went to Okitsu to see Sarah before she left. Janes described the journey of 115 miles from Tokyo to Okitsu as a parade of small garden-like farms, terraces, rice fields, long radishes hung up to dry, farm houses with thatched roofs, and frequent views of Mount Fuji. Otoshige Fujimori made a ten-hour journey from his farm in Shimousa to meet them. Fujimori was preaching as the McCaleb party arrived at Sarah's small house-church. At the conclusion of his sermon, Fujimori had the pleasure of baptizing the thirteenth convert in what had been an untouched town before Sarah's arrival there fifteen months before. "She has done a good and faithful work and is held in high esteem by all the missionaries, and honored in Okitsu by the populace," Janes wrote in the March 1921 issue of *Word and Work*. In the same paper he noted that "Sister Cypert is in good health, spry as a cricket, and a valuable servant of God."

Sarah had been in Okitsu slightly more than a year, but she had endeared herself to the people to such an extent that the train station was crowded with those who had come to see her off. The hotel keeper, the stationmaster (whose son had accepted Christ), a host of children, and others bid her *sayonara*, bowing repeatedly and waving farewell as the train pulled away from the depot. As the only Christian worker in a town of 8,600 souls, she averaged nearly one convert a month. The local people spoke of her as an angel and had granted her the free use of public property for her work.

After spending the night in Tokyo accompanied by numerous friends, Sarah went on to Yokohama where she boarded the *S.S. Colombia* and arrived in San Francisco January 26. She remained at home for two years until sufficient funds were contributed to pay for her return ticket to Japan in January 1923. Her absence was felt strongly, and the importance of the women's work in Japan was emphasized as Lillie was also home on furlough for part of that time. She had left on the *Korea Maru* on May 25, 1922, arriving in San Francisco on June 11.

Part of Lillie's furlough was spent visiting family in Oak Flat, Arkansas. She also taught classes at the Abilene Mexican Mission. Texas required all children to attend school but the Mexican and U.S. children would not mix. Abilene Christian College saw the opportunity to do mission work in their own backyard and began a school for the Mexican children. When she wasn't teaching, Lillie visited churches in several towns to give a report on the work in Japan and solicit support. Just prior to her return to Japan, she met J. D. Tant who was so impressed with her Christian character that he urged all preachers and churches to support her.

While these two female workers were absent from the field, the Bixlers had moved out of Tokyo to begin a new work in Nagasawa, Ibaraki. E. A. and Bess Rhodes built a house in Omiya, Ibaraki. The Herman Fox family also moved to Ibaraki while the Harry Robert Foxes established work in a new area in Tanakura, Fukishima, leaving McCaleb to carry on the work in Tokyo with just the assistance of elderly Alice Miller. Strong appeals were made in the papers for additional workers for Japan. O. D. Bixler wrote about the work he and his wife were beginning in Nagasawa, the old Wagner–Fujimori homestead. He noted the need for more workers, especially women. "A woman worker is needed to work in the homes of this community. Who will say, 'Here am I?'"

This was part of the purpose of furloughs. Not only did the missionaries need an opportunity to visit family and friends every five to seven years (the standard time frame between furloughs), but it also provided opportunities for the missionaries to speak to individuals in churches and on college campuses in order to build interest in their work. They visited their supporters to thank them for their contributions and secure additional funds. They told of the work they were doing and the results they were seeing. And they tried to stir up interest and build enthusiasm that might result in others deciding to join them on the mission field.

Theological Obstacles

During the next two decades of the 1920s and 1930s, recruiting and financing workers faced an additional obstacle. Differences of opinion that raged in the States, such as the scripturalness of missionary societies or the use of instrumental music, impacted the foreign missionaries in the earlier years. Now hampering the sending and funding of missionaries in the 1920s and 1930s was the premillennial issue. The doctrine had been around in other religious groups since colonial days, but there was a noticeable increase of interest in it following World War I. The war and other disasters had stirred the belief that Christ would return soon to set up his physical, earthly kingdom for a literal thousand years, and the end of time was near.

The issue became divisive within the a cappella Churches of Christ when it was preached and promoted as doctrine by R. H. Boll and his followers. It affected the mission efforts of the church because Boll was the publisher of *Word and Work* and Don Carlos Janes, who wrote the missionary column in the paper, also held the premillennial viewpoint. The *Gospel Advocate* and *Firm Foundation*, on the other hand, represented the majority of the churches in rejecting the theory. When Janes noted a significant decrease in contributions for the missionaries, McCaleb expressed the opinion that Janes and *Word and Work* no longer represented the views of the brotherhood and that was why Christians were not sending funds to the missionaries through Janes.

Churches also scrutinized each potential missionary concerning their "soundness" on the doctrine. Few churches were willing to support a missionary who embraced the premillennial view. In reality, the issue rarely surfaced on the mission field. The missionaries were busy enough teaching the basics of Christianity without broaching the subject of such controversial and nonessential issues. At one point, Sarah Andrews' financial administrator and preacher for her home church in

Dickson, I. B. Bradley, wrote to inquire of her opinion about Boll's views. She assured him that she was opposed to them. To their credit, even though Sarah and her fellow workers did not share their views, Janes and Boll continued to publish reports of the work in Japan and solicit funds for all of the missionaries.

OPPORTUNITIES ABOUND

The opportunities to teach the gospel in Japan seemed to "fall into their lap" at times. On one such occasion, the Japanese offered to equip a kindergarten if the Christians would provide a teacher who would be given full freedom to teach about Christ. Another time a military officer, his brother, and another man came to Nagasaki to request to be baptized. Twelve years earlier, he had found a New Testament floating in the harbor that had been dropped from a ship. He arranged for a Chinese translation of the English Bible, as he could read Chinese but not English. Reading the Testament resulted in his desire for baptism. Indeed, the fields were white for harvest but the laborers were few.

As Lillie prepared to return to Japan at the end of her furlough, the appeal was made again in *Word and Work*: "Bro. O. D. Bixler wants a woman to assist in the country work. A missionary for Tokyo is also needed—in fact a half dozen persons are needed this very year. Who wants to go out as Sister Cypert returns?" Apparently Lillie's speaking appointments while on furlough brought some results as A. C. Miller in Waxahachie, Texas, wrote, "We had the pleasure of hearing the brother who has been in Japan. Interest in missions was helped by him and Miss Cypert."

Bess Rhodes, who was serving in Japan with her husband, wrote an emotional request as well. "When I think of the many that are passing away each day without ever having heard of the true God and of the saving power of Jesus' blood, it makes me cry. Oh that the churches in America would wake up and realize the blessed privilege of sending the gospel to them who know Him not—know absolutely nothing about Him, not even His name."

Perhaps it was the distance from home (three weeks travel time by ship), or the uncertainty of financial support, or the difficult language, or the primitive living conditions that discouraged most from considering Japan as a field of work. When Sarah arrived back in Japan at the end of her furlough in January 1923, efforts were begun to eliminate one obstacle. A building fund had been started in order to secure her a Western-style house. "This faithful woman whose health is not very good should be supplied promptly with the means to provide her a sanitary home," Janes wrote. "Failure here on our part may shorten her life. Please think and act—*promptly.*" The reasoning was explained further in the April *Word and Work.* "More Japanese are said to die annually from tuberculosis than were killed in the Russo-Japanese War— another reason why Sister Andrews and all our workers should have American style houses." Considering how many missionaries suffered from tuberculosis, the request was not unreasonable.

The work was not dependent on missionary housing or church buildings, however. Some of their most effective evangelism took place in public parks. Street preaching was a common method of evangelism used by the missionaries. A Japanese brother usually stood on the street corner to invite people to enter the park while the missionary preached and others handed out tracts amongst the crowd. A group of Christians, including Sarah, gathered in a park on one occasion in the spring of 1923 and began singing. As crowds gathered, the Christians announced that anyone who wanted a Bible could have one without cost. In a matter of minutes they gave away 150 Bibles. With the aid of local officials they were directed to fifty destitute families and gave them food and clothing. Later, Sarah returned with more blankets for the needy.

DISASTER RELIEF

The work of building houses for the missionaries was slowed, however, following the disastrous earthquake in September 1923. With so much devastation in Tokyo, Yokohama, and the surrounding area, it was more urgent to see to the immediate needs of the people. Lillie was still on furlough when the earthquake struck, but Sarah was at her home in Okitsu, one hundred miles north of Tokyo. Bixler, in Karuizawa, was about the same distance from the epicenter and described it as rocking the train he was on from side to side so forcibly that he expected it to jump the track. "I jumped off and started for home on the run, but in only a moment the second shock came and the earth trembled and danced under my feet until I tottered like a drunken man," he said. "The buildings groaned and the poles swayed till it seemed the electric wires must break—and maybe electrocute us."

McCaleb, concerned about Sarah, made the one hundred–mile journey to Okitsu to be sure she was safe. He found that she had escaped injury as she had been resting at a hot springs across Suruga Bay from Okitsu when the quake struck. She was typing school lessons when she felt the first shock. She and Iki san ran from the house clinging to each other as the ground moved in waves beneath their feet. The night passed with them running in and out of the house as the aftershocks continued. They could hear the ground rumbling in the mountains nearby.

In Tokyo, McCaleb's house was damaged and another missionary's home had the chimney top go through the floor. One of the church buildings had to be propped, and McCaleb's dormitory had the roof partly shaken off while the Foxes' house was completely unroofed. As a result, Don Carlos Janes begged for funds in his missionary column, pointing out the great need to secure safe and sanitary housing for the missionaries so that they could carry on the work of the gospel as well as provide physical relief among the earthquake victims. "The lives of the missionaries (at the least, their physical health and usefulness) are involved and that means the salvation of souls is at stake," he explained.

The churches in the United States responded to the destitute people of Japan, and Sarah received a check for $488.09 sent by J. C. McQuiddy, editor of the *Gospel Advocate.* She fell on her knees and thanked God for the generosity of her Christian family. Sarah and McCaleb, with the help of Iki san, set about distributing clothing and household items to the earthquake victims. They also took the opportunity to distribute tracts and preach. They handed out 328 Bibles and guessed that at least ten thousand people heard the gospel.

The following month, Fujimori and another Japanese preacher, Yunosuke Hiratsuka, came to Okitsu to conduct a five-day meeting. Hiratsuka was a descendant of a samurai warrior but was converted by McCaleb and appointed by William Bishop as an elder in the Kamitomizaka church. They set up a tent on a vacant lot and used planks donated by a local lumber mill for seats. The results were eighteen baptisms, a record for a single meeting in Japan.

LILLIE RETURNS TO DEVASTATION

Lillie, eager to get back to her work in Japan, sailed two months after the quake. She arrived in Yokohama on December 18 and wrote the following description of what she saw:

> We had been peering through our field glasses for hours to see the ruined city, and a desolation it is, nothing left to make it look like the place I sailed from less than a year and a half before. A great crowd stood on the broken pier, with eager faces to welcome back to the stricken homeland, friends and loved ones, many of whom had lost homes and even friends and relatives in the great disaster.
>
> As we neared the landing I searched the crowd with my field glasses for familiar faces, and at last I found Ogawa san (my former helper), her friend, and her brother. After a greeting and a little further search, I found Brother McCaleb. They had been waiting since about ten o'clock that morning. It was then about four in the afternoon. The baggage could not be taken off and inspected in the usual way, so it was dark before we left the pier, getting the baggage to the station and getting it checked and off on the train to Tokyo was no small task where conveniences are so meager.
>
> It was ten o'clock that night before we got home. I call the place where my few household goods are home. They are in a little Japanese house outside of the city limits but a very crowded section. Fortunately, however, in a section that was untouched by the fire, and damaged but little by the earthquake. My things are generally all right, only a few picture frames broken. The next day I had my baggage brought over from the station, and prepared to go to see Sister Andrews, as she had sent for me to come. I spent the next eight days with her, we had a quiet but pleasant Christmas together.

I came back to Tokyo on the 29th and have been doing what I could since to get started in my work. I am still in the little Japanese house, and it is so cold I can hardly get on clothes enough to keep from freezing. Am just getting over a severe cold. The first one I have had since before I left Japan in 1922. Thanks to the church in San Francisco for the nice little coal oil stove you gave me the money to buy. It certainly is a necessity out here where we have no gas, and in a Japanese house where we can use neither wood nor coal.

A House For Sarah

The added benevolent work and the cold winter took a toll on Sarah's health and she was reported sick in bed in February 1924. "She should be in a better house," was the prognosis. Worship services were conducted in a tent with good results, however.

McCaleb had begun a building fund to be able to have Western-style houses built for each of the missionary families. Sarah's brother Pete was especially concerned about Sarah's living conditions. He found that Sears and Roebuck advertised a house kit in their catalog. "Aunt Mag" Lipscomb was also concerned. While Sarah had been home in 1922, she became well acquainted with David Lipscomb's widow. In addition to giving Sarah a hot water bottle to keep her warm in the cold Japanese winters, she mounted a campaign to buy Sarah a house. Finally in the spring of 1924, funds from family and friends were sufficient for Sarah to order a pre-fab house to be shipped over from Oregon and assembled in Shizuoka, a city where she had opened a new work twelve miles west of Okitsu.

Sarah's family believes it was one of the Sears kits that Sarah received. The Sears catalogue of pre-fab homes available then includes a model that roughly resembles the floor plan that Harry Robert Fox Jr. recalls for Sarah's home. Historian Earl West, however, wrote that the house was from the Alladin Company of Portland, Oregon. He identified it as a model called "Victory" and says that Sarah liked the name so much she continued to call it that.

Whichever house it was, the pre-fab structure was sent on a ship from Portland with each piece numbered for assembly. There was only one problem—the instructions were written in English and the workers Sarah hired to assemble the house could not read English. Each day she went to the work site to translate the instructions for the work that day. She was pleased when the job was done with "only a few pieces left over." It was especially appreciated that the house was wired for electricity since she only had candlelight previously. The church began meeting in her home in October 1926.

Two other houses were ordered at the same time for twin brothers Harry and Herman Fox and their families, who were serving in Fukushima and Tokyo. It was estimated that the cost for those two houses would be $3,158 plus inland shipping, land, foundations, and assemblage fees. One of the women missionaries who wished

J.M. McCaleb's house constructed in Tokyo.
Photo courtesy of Yukikazu Obata

to remain anonymous wrote, "No one knows how thankful we would be to have even the humblest of foreign (American-style) houses. Japanese kitchens are so inconvenient and of course as cold as ice."

The Japanese Exclusion Act

The gospel work in Japan suffered a setback early in 1924 when the U.S. Congress passed The Immigration Act, or, as it was known in Japan, The Japanese Exclusion Act. Under this law virtually all immigration from Japan was halted. Since Japan and the United States had had an amiable relationship and encouraged immigration since 1907, the Japanese were angry. Nellie Straiton, Lillie's main financial administrator at the time, remarked, "When the great earthquake of September, 1923, brought desolation to hundreds of thousands in Tokyo and elsewhere, the American people very kindly sent gifts of money, food, and clothing, and the people of Japan attributed this generosity to Christianity and were more favorably inclined to the acceptance of the Gospel of Christ. But when The Exclusion Act was passed by Congress the Japanese people 'lost their confidence and decided that the help they had received was only deceitfulness and that the Christian religion was the prompter' of the immigration law also. As a result where formerly there was interest manifested in the teaching of our Bible now there is indifference and prejudice."

Even R. H. Boll expressed concern about the backlash of sentiment the missionaries would encounter when he wrote, "Pray for the Japanese missionaries. The resentment stirred up in Japan because of the anti-Japanese legislation, excluding the Japanese from our shores, is sure to bring trouble to our missionaries. There is a bitter feeling against Americans over there, which has already, so it is reported, broken out in mob-violence in some parts. The situation constitutes a special call to prayer. It is understood that we should constantly sustain our missionaries with our prayers. But now there is a special need. . . . Let us pray for McCaleb and for Rhodes and Bixler, and Harry and Herman Fox and their wives and little ones; also for Sister Cypert and Sister Andrews—that God may graciously protect them, and continue to give them an open door for the Gospel."

Their prayers were answered in one aspect as two new workers decided to enter the work that fall. Clara Kennedy set sail in August 1924 at the same time Hettie Lee Ewing announced her intentions to join those on the field, although it would be another two years before Hettie Lee arrived. A request was also made for $150 to purchase a typewriter and other equipment for Clara to take with her.

CHAPTER FIFTEEN

MORE LABORERS FOR THE HARVEST

At the conclusion of 1924, J. M. McCaleb reported the results of all combined efforts of the independent missionaries since their beginnings in 1892: twelve missionaries in the field, nine Japanese evangelists, ten Sunday schools, nineteen teachers, eleven churches, ten preaching stations, two kindergartens, one training school, four church buildings, and eight missionary homes. It didn't seem like much to show for thirty-two years of labor. In other news, Lillie Cypert bought herself a bicycle to be able to make her visits more easily, and Sarah Andrews was under the weather again.

The news as reported by Nellie Straiton was more encouraging. "The number in attendance at the Zoshigaya Sunday School, of which Sister Cypert has charge, has been increasing until now there are one hundred enrolled," she wrote.

Sister Cypert has a Teachers Meeting every week at which time she teaches the lesson to these Japanese Christians, which they in turn teach to the little folks on the following Sunday. Thus, in preparing the lesson to teach the children, they are really learning themselves. Early in the year she also assisted in a Sunday School for the earthquake sufferers which was held in the barracks where these refugees were housed.

One of the Ladies Bible Classes which Sister Cypert conducted during 1924 met regularly every week in a study of the Bible by a very simple outline which they enjoyed very much. The study hour was followed by interesting lessons in American sewing or cooking. Not even the hot summer months could break up the interest in this class. . . . There were also other classes in Bible study and in English.

Some money was contributed specifically for the Kindergarten but most of the expense of equipping it was met out of Sister Cypert's personal funds. It opened on September 15th with thirty pupils and two teachers, and before the close of the year there were thirty-nine enrolled. The work among these little folks is very interesting, and through them Sister Cypert is given an opportunity to meet their parents and perhaps through time to tell them the Story of the Savior. The tuition almost pays the teachers, but more funds are needed for better equipment.

Lillie gained some much-needed assistance from two Japanese helpers, a young man and a young woman, who were especially close to her. Kensho Yanai and Kame Ogawa began helping Lillie in the Sunday school. Kame was a student and needed an older person to guide her. Lillie took her into her home and taught her the gospel. She aided Lillie in the Sunday school and the translation work. Yanai also helped translate the Sunday school material from English to Japanese. The two young people were married before Lillie's first furlough. When Yanai went to fulfill the mandatory military training, Kame and their new baby lived with Lillie. Over the years, Lillie became like a mother to the Yanai children. Several years later, Lillie helped the youngest child, Steve, enter Pepperdine College in Los Angeles to study religion.

Although her first experience with a girls' boarding school had ended in failure a few years earlier, Lillie was hopeful of better results the second time. Early in 1925, she opened the Girls' Training School at Zoshigaya, a section of Tokyo, using part of the Zoshigaya church building for the dormitory that had been damaged by the earthquake. She and her Bible woman Kame lived in the dormitory and hired two additional teachers. Kame and a Korean boy cleaned the building and assisted with other repairs.

It was reported that Lillie used her own personal funds to finance the work along with some donations from her supporters back home. It was expected that the school tuition would cover the teachers' salaries in time. Until then, help was solicited to provide sixty dollars per month for two teachers. Bible, English, cooking, and sewing were to be part of the curriculum in addition to the kindergarten already in operation. Her objective was to train young women for mission work among their own people.

When spring approached, Lillie took her furlough home in order to escape the hot, humid Tokyo summer. She arrived in San Francisco on board the *Siberia Maru* on May 16, 1925, and went directly to Porterville, California, where her mother, stepfather, and sister Sadie had moved. When the summer had passed, she sailed back to Japan on August 18 in company with George and Sally Benson and Barney and Nellie Morehead . The Bensons went on to China where they labored for many years. The Moreheads made Japan their base of operation.

SARAH'S HEALTH FAILS AGAIN

While Lillie had been gone, Sarah's health declined further. She was reported in May to be "seriously sick" and faced the possibility of returning from the field. She spent several weeks in Tokyo and Tanakura where she stayed with Harry Robert Fox and his family, then continued on to Hokkaido, the northern island of Japan, hoping to regain her health. "I may have to go (home)," Sarah wrote, "and will if it seems best later on, though as far as my wishes are concerned I would love to go to heaven from Japan." This became a mantra for Sarah as family and friends recalled various occasions when she informed them that heaven was just as near Japan as Tennessee. "She does not regard going to the mission field as so great a sacrifice as being compelled to relinquish the work," Janes observed. It wasn't until April of the following year that Janes was able to report that Sarah's health had improved. She had been sidelined for nearly an entire year.

In the summer of 1926, Sarah found it necessary to suspend her teaching load while trying to do some writing and studying. The break aided her return to health, too. "Guess I was more tired than I realized for since I have freedom from class responsibility my appetite is better and I may be gaining weight," she noted. "The Lord is good to me."

Iki san, her faithful companion, had also been ill, and Sarah felt as if she had lost her right hand during that time. She also incurred unexpected expenses and noted at the end of the year that she wondered how she had managed.

Although Sarah reported that she felt much stronger and regained mobility, the improvement in her health was only temporary and declined again during the winter months. In February 1927, Bradley announced in the *Gospel Advocate* that Sarah's physicians had advised her to return home to rest and recuperate. "She was frail to begin with," Bradley explained, "and the treacherous climate of Japan, together with the hardships incident to the work, has undermined her health, and she has been compelled to do a great deal of her work during the past two years under very trying conditions—a great deal of the time from her room, and in some cases from her bed, giving directions to her assistants."

Iki san would be coming with her on this trip to look after her and would receive a break from the routine of her work in the mission. Bradley assured Sarah's supporters that even though she was coming back only four years since her last furlough, her health demanded it. "She is an untiring, conscientious worker and an efficient missionary," he told them. "She has done a great work, and it is a great pity that she has to give it up even to come home for recuperation. But she is too good a servant to not try to recover her strength and keep on with the work." This was followed by his usual appeal for funds in order to purchase the ship tickets.

On June 16, 1927, Sarah and Iki san headed for home on the *Arizona Maru*. Sarah said it was harder to leave this time. Her co-workers gathered on the dock to see her off. Together they sang, "God Be with You till We Meet Again." More prayers were requested for the recovery of "this most devoted woman." "I want to get well for service," she wrote a year later. To take her place, Hettie Lee Ewing was scheduled to arrive in Japan in August and would stay in Sarah's house while she was gone.

ANOTHER WOMAN FOR THE WORK

Hettie Lee made her decision to go to Japan in response to a letter from Lillie. Hettie Lee was in attendance at a meeting of the Furman Avenue Church of Christ near Corpus Christi, Texas, in May 1924. O. E. Phillips, from Abilene, finished his sermon and then read a letter from Lillie, who was begging for Phillips to find some-one about her age to come to Japan and work with her. Hettie Lee recalled thinking, "Maybe, maybe that is my call. Maybe I should go. Maybe I'm the one."

She arranged for a meeting with Phillips for the purpose of discussing the possibility of answering Lillie's plea. Reluctantly and fearfully, she broached the subject as their meeting was nearly at an end and he was preparing to leave. "Sister Cypert's letter appealed to me," she explained, "and I have been thinking for a long time I would so like to go and help to teach the Bible in a land where the Bible is not very well known." Phillips was pleased with her interest and encouraged her against her fears.

Hettie Lee had grown up with an emotionally distant and verbally abusive father after her mother's death and lacked self-confidence. She had desired to be a teacher, but her father convinced her she was too stupid to pass the examination for a teaching certificate. Indeed, she failed it three times before finally acquiring the license.

Hettie Lee Ewing
Photo courtesy of Disciples of Christ Historical Society

Now she was sure she would never be able to learn the Japanese language, but Phillips assured her that once she was in the country she would be able to master it.

As Phillips concluded the Gospel Meeting he was conducting for the church that week, he announced Hettie Lee's decision to the congregation. Once it became a public matter, there was no way for her to back down. But there was one major obstacle in her way—her father. He had never approved of her getting an education or becoming a teacher, and she anticipated his reaction to this new venture. In addition, he depended on her for his care. She prayed for God to open a way for her to go, and even if she could only do a little, she would remember the words of the Lord about the woman who bathed his feet and anointed them with oil. "If I could only hear my Savior say, in the end, 'She did what she could,' I thought, that would be recompense enough."

She set a goal for herself to save her money and sell her car and a few other things for the funds to go to Japan within a year, but she worried about how to inform her father. During the first few weeks of that year her father took a vacation to another town and sent a letter back to her informing her that he had found a good woman there whom he had decided to marry. "The first great hurdle in my pathway had been removed," Hettie Lee felt. "I didn't have to worry any more about what would happen to my father if I went a long way off, to Japan."

Her next step was provided by Sam Hall, a preacher in Nashville who had a great interest in the Japanese mission in Los Angeles. Hall arranged for her to go to Los Angeles to spend a year at the Westside Church of Christ with Hirosuke Ishiguro, who would begin to acclimate her to the culture and language. As the end of her year in Los Angeles drew to a close, she still had not secured her travel funds to Japan. She was faced with the alternate decision to abandon her missionary plans and seek a teaching position in the States. Then just as unexpectedly as the letter from her father had arrived, she received another letter from Sam Hall. "Sister Ewing," he wrote, "you may go downtown and buy yourself a trunk because I'm sending you a $300 check to send you out to Japan."

The money was a gift from Cora M. Brooks of Baltimore, Maryland. She inherited it and wanted it used to spread the gospel. A young Japanese lady whom she dearly loved worked in Brooks' home as a maid. Their relationship prompted her investment. Besides the three hundred dollars Hall sent to Hettie Lee, he also sent a portion of Cora Brooks' "investment" to Sarah, and the remainder was used to purchase a building for the Japanese Westside Church.

Finally, on August 13, 1926, Hettie Lee boarded the *Siberia Maru* and embarked for Japan. She shared a cabin in tourist class with Ethel Mattley, a Church of Christ missionary who was on her way back to China. They reached Yokohama on September 2 where they were met by McCaleb, Lillie, and the Moreheads. Clara Kennedy joined them the next day on an excursion around the city of Tokyo.

CHAPTER SIXTEEN

GAINS AND LOSSES

On June 16, 1927, Sarah boarded the *Arizona Maru* with Iki san and headed to the United States for "an operation and a needed rest." As she departed Japan, she told her friends, "Some folks may think and talk of being in Japan as a sacrifice, but to me leaving is the supreme sacrifice." The two women arrived in Seattle on June 27. She spent the first few weeks in Colorado Springs to take advantage of the high altitude. When this didn't produce an improvement in her health, she went to visit the Mayo Clinic in Rochester, Minnesota, for a complete physical examination.

Dr. Charles H. Mayo invited her to come with the assurance it would only take three or four days. At the end of three weeks, she was still undergoing tests. Another three weeks and more exams revealed that there were too many problems. To begin with, she had "author-ities" (arthritis), an intestinal parasite that had caused her weight to drop significantly, and discomfort in her chest caused by heart muscles. Dr. Mayo believed she was very close to a nervous breakdown.

Sarah was relieved of one worry at least when Dr. Mayo informed her that there would be no cost for their doctors or clinic fees as they didn't charge missionaries.

Sarah's mother and a sister lived in Lakeland, Florida, where Sarah intended to rest in the warm Florida sunshine after a stay in Nashville. While Sarah was in Florida, Iki san enrolled at David Lipscomb College for the fall semester, and when the next summer came they reunited and journeyed together to Southern California to assist with the Japanese work at the Westside Church of Christ. "I try to be resigned to these periods of inactivity," she wrote from Los Angeles.

When Sarah's health showed no signs of returning by the time they moved to Los Angeles, George Pepperdine sent his family doctor to look after her at his own expense. This physician believed there was some indefinable problem with her lungs. He insisted that she take treatments at his office three times a week at a cost of forty to fifty dollars per month. Even though Pepperdine was paying the bill, Sarah worried about the high cost and was very grateful to Pepperdine for his interest and assistance.

Anticipating that Sarah's new house in Shizuoka City would be empty while she was gone, Hettie Lee was asked to move into it in Sarah's absence. The Okitsu church that Sarah had established was about thirty minutes by train from the house, but there was no Church of Christ in the town of Okitsu itself. Two Christians whom Sarah had taught and Fujimori had baptized—a brother and sister, Kinji and Michiko Tashiro—lived in the town. They had been Christians several years and agreed to help Hettie Lee begin a Sunday school and Bible classes in Okitsu. Sarah's house had a Japanese-style guesthouse in the rear, and Hettie Lee convinced the siblings to move into it along with their mother and father.

Hettie Lee dove into the work and was soon teaching several English Bible classes, a Sunday evening Bible class, and taking language lessons. Struggling in the language school, it wasn't long before she withdrew and opted to learn the language "on the street" by visiting shops and mingling with the people.

LILLIE'S OUTREACH EFFORTS

When Lillie initiated the second attempt at a school for girls in 1925, J. M. McCaleb turned his dormitory building over to her. The building had been damaged in the earthquake of 1923, but was usable for a kindergarten until more extensive repairs could be done. Lillie employed a local woman to serve as matron and opened the Girls' Training School. It did not work out well, though, when Lillie had a disagreement with McCaleb about how the work was to be carried out. She decided to turn the work in Zoshigaya over to McCaleb and began a work in Kichijoji, eight miles west of Zoshigaya.

She arranged for a building to be constructed that was completed on November 10, 1927. In accordance with Japanese custom, it was built on rented land consisting of just over an acre and cost $250 down and $12.50 per month. There was a chapel on one end that would seat about seventy in a room 15 x 27 feet. On the other end were the kindergarten room, 15 x 21 feet, and a second classroom 9 x 12. Between the two ends were her living quarters and more classrooms.

Her kindergarten opened on April 29, 1929, with 150 children. Lillie wrote a lengthy account of her work in Kichijoji that was published in May 1929.

> On November 12, 1927, we had our first meeting. At that time there were only four of us members to take communion, Mr Yanai, my co-worker and preacher; his wife, Miss Kamioki, the kindergarten teacher, and myself. In January we realized the first fruits of our labor in a young man being baptized into Christ. During the year 1928, twelve were added by baptism and

Lillie Cypert (back row with fur collar) and one of her kindergarten classes.
Photo courtesy of Steve Yanai

one by membership, making a total of seventeen members. This year, thus far, three have been baptized. All of these are faithful and working.... Three more have confessed their faith in Him and have asked for baptism on next Sunday. Others are diligently searching the Scriptures to see if these things are true.

From the beginning we have had a Bible school of about fifty children and a weekly ladies' Bible class with an average of ten members. We began the kindergarten with six children enrolled and only three present and one teacher. We now have twenty-six enrolled, and two teachers. We give them daily teaching and have a monthly mothers' meeting.

In March of last year we began to do some street preaching and giving out of literature in a nearby village. In August we rented a hall and began regular meetings on Friday afternoon for the children and in the evening for grown-ups. We now have an enrollment in the Bible school of over one hundred and fifty children and have had to enlarge our quarters, which we could do conveniently by renting a small warehouse that stood nearby.

From the meetings for the grown-ups, three have been baptized, two of whom are primary school teachers, thus giving the hundreds of children they are teaching Christian influence.

She announced her intention to begin a kindergarten the next month in order to have the children six days a week instead of just one day, plus access to their homes with an opportunity to teach the mothers. Her article concluded with an account of her expenditures and income and an appeal for additional funds to cover the expenses of the school.

George Pepperdine Appeals for Missionary Support

Lillie mentioned receiving forty-five dollars per month beginning in June 1928 from "Brother Pepperdine's mission extension fund." This resulted from a visit George Pepperdine made in 1928 when he spent almost a month in Japan visiting all the places of mission work and studying the needs and conditions. He came to the conclusion that the work of a missionary was no small undertaking. He stated, "The most difficult task ever given to mortal man is the spreading of the gospel in heathen lands."

He followed his conviction with a commitment. "I have resolved," he said, "to invest several thousand dollars of my own money each year in this great Scriptural work and to put forth some real effort during the rest of my life to get our churches in general to wake up to this urgent need and to their responsibility. . . ."

An immediate result of Pepperdine's visit was his fund-raising plan that he called, "A Prayer and a Penny a Day." In the December 1928 issue of *Word and Work*, the savvy businessman who made a fortune with his Western Auto Supply stores unveiled a plan to raise money to support more missionaries.

"Since my recent report on 'Missionary Work in Japan' appeared in some of the Church papers," he explained, "a number of people have expressed their desire to give a little money in a systematic way for mission work. The great need of the Gospel of Christ in heathen lands is beginning to make an impression upon the conscience of many Christians. If we take advantage of this opportunity by encouraging people to begin at once their giving to mission work, we can provide better support for our missionaries already in the field and send several other couples who have volunteered to go."

"Friends," he continued, "we ought to take the matter of missionary work seriously. The horrible and hopeless condition of people living in lands where Jesus and His gospel are not known should weigh upon our conscience. The word of Jesus in the great commission, 'Go ye therefore and teach all nations,' is still binding upon us and we cannot safely turn a deaf ear to the call of our unfortunate brothers who have had no opportunity to hear the gospel and embrace it. In our own country everyone has an opportunity to hear and obey if they will, but many spurn the appeal. Our obligation to them is great, but not as great as to those who have never heard of Jesus the Saviour, and God the Father whose love can redeem sinners."

Pepperdine proposed a solution. "In order to make a definite start in this direction, I have prepared cards for individual members of the church to sign, indicating their interest in mission work and their resolution to help. The card is reprinted herewith:"

George Pepperdine (front center) took his mother (on his right) on a world tour in 1928. In Omiya, Ibaraki, they had this photo taken with the Church of Christ missionaries in Japan at that time. Back row (l-r): Harry Robert Fox Sr. (holding Jean Fox), Anna Bixler, O. D. Bixler, J. M. McCaleb, Clara Kennedy, unknown, Nellie Morehead, B. D. Morehead, Ryushi Ebine, Yunosuke Hiratsuka, Herman Fox, Otoshige Fujimori, E. A. Rhodes, Iki Naemura. Seated adults (l-r): Pauline Fox, Lillie Cypert, Hettie Lee Ewing, Mary Pepperdine, George Pepperdine, Sarah Fox, Bess Rhodes. Children (l-r): Harry Robert Fox Jr., Sterling Fox, Logan Fox, Elizabeth Fox, Ramona Fox, Martha Fox, Evelyn Fox, William Fox, Erroll Rhodes, Robert Rhodes.

Photo courtesy of Harry Robert Fox Jr.

"A PRAYER AND A PENNY A DAY"
For Missionary Work

I realize the great need of the Gospel and the love of Christ among the people who are in darkness in heathen lands. I am grateful to God for His blessings to me; for the Bible and sufficient intelligence to read and appreciate it, for the association of Christian friends in this glorious land of Christian civilization and Churches of Christ.

In order to show my appreciation to God and to do my bit toward spreading the Gospel of Christ in other lands, I have resolved that in the future I will each day give at least one instant to prayerful thought, in silent prayer, for the success of our missionaries in foreign lands. I will also give of my means an average of at least one cent per day for mission work in addition to my regular gifts to the Church. This special gift of one cent per day, 30¢ per month, (or more if I am able) will be given to the treasurer of the Church to which I belong with a request to place it in a special fund for mission work. If no such fund exists I will send it to a Church of Christ which is doing missionary work.

Signed: _____

Address: _____

This card to be given to treasurer of the church
with first gift. If you are able to give 3¢ or 10¢
per day ($1.00 or $3.00 per month, or more) state
amount here _____ ($ _____ per month).

He agreed to provide a supply of these cards to any church that would use them. Later he established the Pepperdine Foundation, overseen by the Southwest Church of Christ in Los Angeles where he was an elder. By having the church administer the funds, he could avoid the accusation that he had created a missionary society of his own.

The May 1932 issue of *Word and Work* carried three letters aimed at enlarging the force of workers on foreign fields. The first letter was signed by four of those serving in Japan—B. D. Morehead, Lillie Cypert, J. M. McCaleb and E. A. Rhodes. George Benson in China, Max Langpaap in Hawaii, and H. G. Cassell in the Philippines also added their names. The letter was a reminder of Pepperdine's plan. "The nominal daily gift of a cent apiece to this work would support a thousand missionaries nicely. The meager average of 10 cents as a special gift from each member once a year would supply $50,000 for travel money and housing. There are perhaps 5,500 churches of Christ in U.S. abstaining from the great innovations which have divided the church, and though regarding themselves 'loyal' have no part in this scripturally bound work." This was a pointed remark aimed at those who opposed organized missionary societies but were still not contributing directly to mission work.

The second letter was from four Christian businessmen—A. L. Whitelaw (Burroughs Adding Machine Co.), E. E. Beck (Marshall Field and Co.), George Pepperdine (Western Auto Supply Co.), and Clinton Davidson (Estate Planning Corp.). They made their appeal from a business sense. "As Christian business men, we express our desire for the observance of the Lord's will on foreign missionary work by all the congregations of Christ. As the great majority of the churches have not taken up this work, there is a tremendous loss of power which should be remedied. A firm with five-sixths of its members non-productive in the main line of endeavor would be very unbusiness like."

The final letter was signed by four editors of Christian papers—Homer E. Moore (*The Christian Worker*), R. H. Boll, (*Word and Work*), Don Carlos Janes (*The Missionary Messenger*), and Arthur Slater (*Old Paths*). Representing different positions on various issues in the brotherhood at the time, they were careful to limit their appeal to encouraging all "undenominational Christians, churches of Christ," to be "guided by the Book" in their support of missionary work at home and abroad.

A Bitter Loss

As a result of his visit to Japan, Pepperdine offered to take two young men to the United States for training for the ministry. One was Kensho Yanai, Lillie's native helper, and the other was Hettie Lee's helper and friend, Kinji Tashiro. Hettie Lee wanted them to study at Abilene Christian College, but Pepperdine desired for them to be trained in Los Angeles. He had not yet founded George Pepperdine College (now Pepperdine University). Hettie Lee accompanied the two young men, providing supervision, going to classes with them, and helping with their reading and studying for exams during the first year of their training. She returned to Japan in August 1930 while Tashiro and Yanai received one more year of training, returning in the spring of 1931.

Upon returning to his homeland, Tashiro, his sister, and Hettie Lee made plans to work together. In June, a new couple, Carl and Grace Etter, had arrived and asked Hettie Lee and her two helpers to assist them in starting a mission work in the northern island of Hokkaido. By September, a typhoid epidemic swept the island, and Tashiro and his sister both contracted it. Michiko recovered, but Kinji Tashiro died October 15. Hettie Lee described it as the greatest disappointment she had ever suffered.

If one reads between the lines of Hettie Lee's autobiography, one could draw the conclusion that she had a romantic attraction to the young Japanese preacher. She described him as "an attractive young man" with a "million-dollar smile." As early as 1928, after less than two years in Japan, she wrote, "If Sister Andrews had reached no other soul in Japan but Tashiro san, her time would have been well spent for his life is a living sermon." After his death, she confided to one of her students "how precious he [Kinji] had been" to her and that she did not ever want to hope for anything ever again "because it hurts too much when hope is taken away." She even ascribed the departure of another missionary family, the Etters, to their disappointment about his death—perhaps a projection upon them of her own disappointment. One of her nephews observed years later that when Hettie Lee and Tashiro visited in his home, he wondered if he might one day have a Japanese uncle.

Hettie Lee witnessed the cremation of Tashiro's body (the usual procedure following death in Japan) and assisted his aged parents place the ashes in an urn for burial. This was an honor that was reserved only for the nearest of kin, but Hettie Lee requested that they allow her to help them.

Sarah arrived back in Japan about this same time and moved back into her house in Shizuoka City. Hettie Lee moved to the southeast part of the city. Lillie headed for the States on furlough while McCaleb sailed from Vancouver, British Columbia, back to Japan. Their ships would have passed each other going in opposite directions. It seemed there was always someone either coming or going among the missionaries as their furloughs rarely coincided. This was actually a blessing to the work as it would have been much harder on the few who were left if more than one or two missionaries were away at once. Even when they were all in Japan at the same time, the workers were too few for the task. How much could a dozen people do among a country of over fifty million?

A Children's Teacher Needed

Several of the married missionaries had a number of young children who had come with them or been born in Japan. The problem concerning their education began to loom. Appeals were made in *Word and Work* for someone to come to teach the missionaries' children.

This need was answered in the person of Christine Jones. She was recruited to serve as a teacher for the children of the independent missionaries beginning in July 1931. *Word and Work* encouraged this aspect of missionary work, reporting, "She is doing a very important work which gives the children educational advantages. Who knows but that some of these children, reared in Japan, will become efficient workers. They will be better prepared for real efficient service than their parents, as they will know the people. A school in Japan for missionary children will encourage some to go with children. God's blessing upon this work!"

Christine had ten of the missionaries' children in her classes during her first six months and two more were added when E. A. and Bess Rhodes returned with their children from furlough the following month. Christine wrote, "I am happy to be here." She was also involved with the Bible classes held in the evenings for girls.

Christine observed that the native young woman who conducted the Bible study had more faith and zeal than the majority of girls she knew in the States who were raised in Christian homes. The evening classes were for the purpose of teaching hymns and a Bible lesson and then Christine would present an English lesson. The

Japanese were especially anxious to learn the English language. Christine taught the girls to sing "Jesus Loves Me" in English while she was trying to learn to speak Japanese herself. Since she was conducting school for the children all day, she was unable to attend a language school—a situation that made it more difficult for her to learn the complex language. Nevertheless, she had proven herself to be very valuable as a teacher of the missionary children.

Unfortunately in September 1932, McCaleb reported in *Work and Work* that Christine was going to have to return home. "Dr. Gornen Nunro, Medical Advisor of Karuizawa Sanitorium, after a careful examination during three weeks which Miss Jones spent in that institution, strongly recommended that she return at once on account of her health. He found she is suffering from neurasthenia due to overwork."

McCaleb continued to explain that Christine was fatigued when she arrived in Japan, having just completed her education at David Lipscomb College while working in order to pay her tuition. The Japanese climate, extremely cold in the winter and extremely hot in the summer, had combined with the demands of teaching twelve children, who were behind in their studies to begin with, and the strain was "a greater task than her physical strength could stand." Christine arrived back in Los Angeles on July 16, 1932. She was only twenty-four years old.

Her absence left the missionary families in Japan with a dilemma as they were once again without a teacher for their children. Consequently, some made the difficult decision to leave the field while others separated their families, sending their wives with the children back to the States while the men remained in Japan.

CHAPTER SEVENTEEN

THE GREAT DEPRESSION

Lillie Cypert was Stateside during most of Christine Jones' tour of duty, having left on October 28, 1930, and returning during the spring of 1932. She spent her furlough visiting her supporting churches and trying to raise more support. The Depression was beginning to be felt in irregular contributions coming to the mission field, and Lillie reported that she was "especially asking for continued regular support and am trying to impress the necessity of giving it regularly and not to switch or stop without telling us about it, and better still not to give up their responsibility unless they can get some other church to take their place."

Sarah Andrews was also facing a financial decline as several churches had dropped their support while she had been home recovering from illness. She found herself so busy with visitors, though, that she had a hard time keeping up with her reports and correspondence. "We have so many callers together with the regular work," she said, "I find it hard to settle myself to writing. I think I'll have to take 2 or 3 days off every 3 or 4 months and go off to some quiet place and write, write, write. I'm glad indeed that the Japanese feel free to call—wouldn't have it otherwise."

Bank closures, forced by the Depression, posed a problem in getting funds to the missionaries. Janes noted that "even New York drafts are now refused in Japan and China and for all we know in Africa and Brazil, too."

"In view of financial depression," Sarah penned in July 1933, "I am especially grateful to you who continue your support. I regret to tell you that the donations sent through Bro. Bradley in January and February were deposited in the Citizens Bank at Dickson, Tennessee, and since the banking crisis in early March that bank has been unable to reopen. Consequently Bro. Bradley had to take the contributions for March and April to clear the check for $68 sent me in January. Moreover he must take the donations this month to clear the check for $35 sent in February. If the gifts this month are insufficient he must take what is lacking out of the June gifts. So he writes, 'I am not sure when I will have anything to send you again.' Of course, this loss is a blow to the work and our plans but we are trying to make the best of the situation and trusting in God's promises. For the sake of the donors I regret very much that your offerings were lost but I believe you understand the situation and will not be discouraged."

Although stretched financially, Sarah continued with her evangelistic efforts. Even McCaleb, perhaps somewhat out of touch with the effects of the Depression, urged more sacrificial giving for the benefit of the missionaries. "When people learn to live more simply and leave off many needless expenses, times will improve," he wrote.

"The work is moving along very well in the three towns where we are laboring in this section," Sarah reported. The three areas where she had begun churches at this time were Okitsu, Oiwa in Shizuoka City, and Ejiri in Shimizu City, all within the Shizuoka Prefecture. "We are much encouraged over the situation at the new station. We are not unmindful however that the devil is ever busy and may at any time stir up strife, if we are not diligent in prayer. The work has grown and the prospects are so great that we together with the members in the three small churches are unable to cope with the situation."

Native Workers Aid in Work

She went on to explain that one of the preachers who had been working with Fujimori was coming down to Shizuoka once a month and had already baptized three people. A fourteen-year-old girl had asked to be baptized, but her father objected

Okitzu Church of Christ, started by Sarah Andrews, continues today.
Photo courtesy of Yukikazu Obata

and removed his daughter from the assembly before they could head to the river. With so much potential, Brother Kakinuma, a minister, and his wife agreed to move temporarily to Shizuoka to be of more help to Sarah. In addition, Tokuo Mazawa and his wife, who were members of the Westside Church of Christ in Los Angeles and originally from Japan, told Sarah they were coming to Okitsu to spend the winter and would help with the work.

"I feel sure the addition of these capable workers to the field here will mean much to lighten my responsibility," Sarah wrote. "I am thankful indeed for I fear I am not physically able to continue at the present rate. But again I recall the precious promise that God has given."

Though finances were low and contributions irregular, the missionaries continued their work as best they could. Hindered by a back injury sustained in the summer of 1932, Sarah entered a sanitarium in September for treatment of pleurisy and exhaustion. She was out of commission for over a month. Hettie Lee was still in the southeast section of Shizuoka City at the close of the summer of 1933 while Sarah labored in the northwest area of the city known as Oiwa. Each month the journals carried news of a few more baptisms. "I am not in a position to say how many baptisms they have had at Oiwa," Hettie Lee wrote concerning Sarah's work, "but they have a new preacher now, and I am sure they have much to be thankful for and to hope for in the coming months."

"We had seven baptisms in May of this year which up to the present is the sumtotal for this year," Hettie Lee reported in September. "The work at our place is all being done in my house and I hardly have a place to lay my head sometimes."Hettie Lee wrote from Shizuoka City in reference to the work she and Tashiro's sister Michiko and Michiko's husband were doing in the southeast section of the city.

"Have just given up my bedroom, and moved in to the servant room," Hettie Lee wrote. "Our Sunday School numbers more than one hundred each Lord's Day, and the membership of the church is sixteen. Considering there was no Christian teaching in this section of the city until we began here a little more than one year ago, we feel that the Lord has surely blessed our efforts."

She went on to describe their thronged meetings, claiming that one hundred children sat on the floor in a space 12 x 18 feet. One can hardly imagine it. "The crowded condition is hard on the members and especially on the one who has to live right in the house with it," Hettie Lee lamented, "having no place to retreat for rest, since there are from five to seven meetings a week, and we must furnish chairs, tables, etc. for the adults, and it keeps me and my servant woman moving all the time."

"I am earnestly asking the Lord to furnish us with money enough for building a cheap and convenient place for the work," she stated. "It would take about $400 to do it, which amount I would gladly borrow and pay back out of my monthly receipts, if I could manage it."

Hettie Lee's desire became reality as McCaleb loaned the money for a small frame building in Nakahara Ward in the southeast section of Shizuoka City. The twenty Christians, give or take a few, who had been worshipping in her rented house pledged to pay back the loan over a period of three years, which they did.

Sarah also had a meeting place erected in the northwest section of Shizuoka City (Oiwa) as well as one in Ejiri and another in Okitsu. With three churches to oversee, Sarah reported a very busy year at the end of 1933. "Two were baptized here last week and one came to the truth from the sects." Sarah was back in Okitsu when she wrote in December, as the winter climate was more tolerable than in Shizuoka. "This is a seacoast town and we enjoy plenty of fresh fish and various sea foods," she informed her readers.

Most of this "Christmas letter" contained information about the growth of the church rather than about her personal health, although she indicated the milder climate enabled her to accomplish more. "I have during the past several weeks been conducting a class here on Monday evenings for Christians. Although it was the only day I had free during the week. I undertook this extra class trusting God for strength and grace."

HETTIE LEE—COLLEGE STUDENT

As 1934 began, the work in Japan appeared to be progressing well in spite of the irregular financial gifts that came their way from their supporters. That spring, Hettie Lee made a decision to do something she had longed to do for years. She wrote to the president of Abilene Christian College, James F. Cox, about the possibility of enrolling in the college. "I know that Abilene Christian College offers half tuition to prospective preachers. I wonder what you could offer to a missionary who has been on the foreign mission field for ten years?" she inquired.

His response was overwhelming. "Everything!" he responded. "Just get yourself over here, and we will not charge you any tuition. You shall get your college education with a major in Bible."

She arrived in Los Angeles the morning of August 13, 1934, on board the *Taiyo Maru* and proceeded to Texas. For the next three and a half years, Hettie Lee would be a student in Abilene Christian College, receiving her B.A degree at the age of forty. She looked back on those years as "the most beautiful and influential years" in all of her life. "It is difficult to express the fullness and richness of my association there with both students and faculty members, because of my being privileged to go to college and because of the joy I had in being able to do my work very well. I received many blessings there, one of which was receiving my degree."

When she returned to Japan in 1937, she was "supported liberally" by the Fifth and Highland Street Church of Christ in Abilene.

While Hettie Lee was in school in Texas, Sarah received the news that her father, Will Andrews, had passed away in September 1934. The Andrews family was especially close and this was a hard situation for Sarah to face so far from home and unable to attend his memorial service.

Lillie's Love For Children

Lillie's work in Kichijoji grew so much that a new kindergarten wing was added to the existing building in 1935. Her work was interrupted that year when she came down with scarlet fever, her first illness in nineteen years in Japan. She had a Western-style house constructed with the money from the "building fund" McCaleb oversaw. Her living quarters were in-between the church meeting place, on one side, and the new kindergarten wing on the other. Within three years of this addition, the kindergarten was self-supporting as was the Sunday school of ninety children. The church was still 75 percent dependent on foreign support, however.

Harry Robert Fox Jr., who spent his childhood in Japan with his missionary parents from 1924 to 1932, remembers visiting Lillie's home. "She paid special attention to me and my younger brother, Logan, and taught us to sing 'How Do Oats and Peas and Barley Grow.' Every time we visited her she would sing that song to us. This confirmed my impression (even at that early age) that she was interested in *all* small children."

The children whom Lillie helped raise also had fond memories of her. The youngest child, Hideyasu ("Steve") recalled that she spoke only Japanese with them. "She was so fluent in Japanese," Steve recalled, "that if you closed your eyes you could not tell whether she was American or Japanese!"

Sarah and Lillie Face Health Issues

In the summer of 1935, *Word and Work* carried a brief statement that "Sarah Andrews will have to return to the States for an operation." This was reiterated in a report concerning her work but with no explanation for the malady. In the announcement that Tokuo Mazawa, a Japanese student at David Lipscomb College, had completed his studies and would soon go to Japan with his wife to take up Sarah's work, it was explained that Sarah's doctor ordered her return. Funds were solicited to aid in the expenses of sending the Mazawas to Japan and bringing Sarah home. "Sister Andrews has labored long and faithfully, handicapped with a frail body; but she has accomplished more than any other missionary the church has on the foreign field," R. S. King wrote. "Truly she is one of God's great women."

The surgery was evidently not an immediate need as Sarah continued to send reports of her work throughout 1935 and was in Tokyo with Iki san during part of that summer. In fact, it wasn't until May 1936, nearly a year after the initial announcement, that Sarah arrived in San Francisco on the *S.S. Colombia*. She would not return until November 1939, more than three years later.

While she was gone, Lillie also began to experience health problems. The first episode involved trachoma, an eye disease spread by contact. Flies and gnats also transmit the infection, and it is the leading cause of blindness worldwide, especially in Asia, Africa, and the Middle East. It may resemble conjunctivitis at first and can be easily treated with antibiotics. However, if left untreated, it can cause corneal scarring and blindness. An appeal was made for extra funds in order for her to receive the needed medications since health insurance was unheard of at that time. Apparently Lillie received the proper treatment, but a year later she suffered what was called a "collapse," possibly a small stroke. Again, funds were requested to assist with the added expense of medical care. She spent the spring of 1939 in a hospital for treatment and relaxation and then went to the mountains for further rest.

The young Yanai child, Steve, whom Lillie helped raise, recalled going to a mountain retreat with her during that summer. "She had what I think was a stroke while she was there," he remembered. "I know she suffered from really high blood pressure. She really wasn't the same afterwards. She recovered physically, but she seemed to become very paranoid." As early as 1928, Lillie reported having "quite a little trouble" because of her blood pressure. *Word and Work* confirmed in 1936 that she was bothered with high blood pressure but it had lowered and she was resting in the Japanese mountains.

The next problem she encountered involved her teeth. Only two months after her "collapse," *Word and Word* reported Lillie had had "a severe time with her teeth. It required two and one-half hours to remove one which had enough poison about it to do her system much damage." For several more months, the paper continued to describe Lillie's ailing health.

POLITICAL CLIMATE CHANGES

Lillie's perceived paranoia wasn't without foundation. The political situation in the world was changing, and it was especially noticeable in Japan where rationing began as early as 1937, about the time Hettie Lee graduated from college and returned to Japan. By 1938, all kinds of metal things such as pins, brads, and paper clips were being rationed as well as clothing and all white materials that could be used for bandages. Cotton materials were bleached in order to make ready for the wounded as Japan went to war with Manchuria, Korea, and later China.

Blackout curtains had to be closed every night. Sunday school and church attendance began to decrease. The odor of sulfur from ammunition factories filled the air. Occasionally, long lines of soldiers were observed on their way to a shrine carrying tiny white boxes containing the remains of dead comrades. "These boxes did not always contain the ashes of the dead," according to Sarah. "More frequently only some personal effect or perhaps a lock of hair which had been left by its owner to be thus enshrined in the event of the inevitable."

The women were trained to work bucket brigades to douse imaginary fires caused by imaginary bombings. By the time Sarah arrived back in Japan in the fall of 1939, foreigners were not allowed to travel any long distances without permission from the police. Even then, the permits were for specific trains at specific times.

Hettie Lee recounted an interrogation by local police after she made an unscheduled change in her plans when returning from a trip. She intended to stay with McCaleb on her way back but changed her mind and stayed with Lillie instead. The police knew she had not stayed the night where she originally indicated, and they knew where she had been instead. "They knew everything that I did on my trip," she recalled. "Traveling soon became unpleasant; the feeling of being watched was chilling."

Hettie Lee became so concerned that she made the decision, against the advice of her fellow missionaries, to return home. She left Japan October 4, 1940, stopping in Honolulu to enroll in two education courses at the teachers' college in order to bring her teaching certificate up to date. In 1941, she resumed her journey and arrived back in the States in February.

CHAPTER EIGHTEEN

THE WAR BEGINS

As part of Japan's preparations for possible war, all residents were required to keep water and sand at their gates in case of possible fires caused by bombs. As it turned out, this was good advice even without war. Earlier in 1940, before Hettie Lee left, the city of Shizuoka where she and Sarah lived, suffered a fire that wiped out about one-sixth of the city. Two Christians were among the 6,500 families whose houses were consumed. Neither Hettie Lee's nor Sarah's houses were involved, and no church property was lost. Sarah busied herself caring for the refugees.

Even though the Japanese were embroiled in war with China and Korea, Sarah found the people still able to think about spiritual things. She reported another baptism in Okitsu in August 1940 and that the "work at the three stations here [Shizouka Prefecture] is moving along very well. . . ."

That year, the Japanese government created the Kyodan, a Japanese confederation of religious bodies. All religions were to be placed under three divisions—Shinto, Buddhist, and Christian. All denominations were combined into one generic Christian church with only native Japanese holding executive positions. The non-instrumental Churches of Christ resisted joining the Kyodan, even at the risk of losing their properties to the Japanese government. To join, they reasoned, would be to abandon their plea for the restoration of New Testament Christianity.

Sarah Andrews (front row, third from right) with one of her women's Bible study groups.
Photo courtesy of Disciples of Christ Historical Society

Most of the churches supported by the United Christian Missionary Society went willingly into the Kyodan, believing it to be their only alternative other than dissolution. It also appeared on the surface to be a move toward Christian unity—a goal of the Restoration Movement. "If they can be united under one head without becoming a tool of the government, it will be good," Mary Lediard Doan reasoned. "But if unification is merely a plan by which the church can be controlled by the state, it might be very dangerous." Sarah, Lillie and McCaleb believed it to be the latter. They saw it as an infringement on church autonomy as well as a total disregard for biblical authority in regards to doctrine.

A few of the independent Churches of Christ entered the Kyodan, some unwittingly and others knowingly. Lillie had tried to make provisions for her kindergarten and the church property before the Kyodan went into effect. The husband of one of her kindergarten teachers was a lawyer whom she trusted. The lawyer drew up some documents concerning the distribution of Lillie's belongings should anything happen to her. However, the lawyer betrayed her and, not understanding the legal language, she signed the document leaving everything to the lawyer. She lost everything she owned including her furniture, a piano, and the Kichijoji church building.

Efforts to overturn the document were futile, and the judge, though sympathetic to Lillie, ruled in favor of the lawyer because Lillie had signed the paper willingly and she could read Japanese.

Sarah began making a study of the law and teaching members of her churches in her home what the New Testament said about the true church. She endeavored to impress upon them that if their churches entered into the federation, they would cease being Churches of Christ. "I encouraged them to stand for the New Testament order and trust God for the consequences, even if they were ordered to disband and must worship God in secret as in days of old Rome." She proudly proclaimed, "The three churches where I labored were determined to do that very thing. . . ."

Only Four Remain

Among the missionaries in Japan from the Restoration Movement, most left before the attack on Pearl Harbor. Hettie Lee, even with her prolonged layover in Honolulu, arrived back in the U.S. in February 1941. McCaleb delayed leaving Japan until October 22 and stopped over for a visit with the church in Hawaii. He left there November 14, just three weeks before the bombing of Pearl Harbor. Sarah and Lillie, however, stated that they had no thought of leaving. They confidently assured McCaleb before he left that they trusted God to take care of them.

Of the four American Restoration Movement missionaries who remained in Japan, all four were single women—Sarah Andrews, Lillie Cypert, Grace Farnham, and Emily Cunningham. All the men and their families retreated to the States before the war started. Early in the morning on December 8, 1941, a neighbor of Sarah's came to tell her that war had been declared between Japan and the United States. Two days later, Sarah was taken by armed guard to the Japanese military headquarters where she was ordered to stop teaching immediately. She regretted this most of all. She was ordered to submit an inventory of all properties "even to the number of pocket handkerchiefs." The government required all property to be turned over to the state, but Sarah refused to relinquish the deeds to the three churches she had established.

One of the officers asked her why she had more than one copy of the Bible, mistaking as Bibles the study notes she had been preparing on Galatians and Ephesians to be translated into Japanese. These manuscripts were taken from her, although she was allowed to keep her Bible. Before being sent to a concentration camp in September 1942, she rewrote the study guide and left it with a Japanese Christian, Sister Hongo, to translate. When the bombings increased, the manuscripts were placed in a basket of clothing and taken to a large warehouse north of the city. The basket, with its contents, was destroyed during the war.

She had also entrusted some family photos and mementos of her mother's to Iki san, who was now married to Mr. Kashiwagi whose family owned a farm in the country. They buried Sarah's box of treasures on the farm but when the bombing began, one of the bombs hit the burial place dead center. Later, Sarah could laugh about it and commented, "That is what it means to store up your treasures in heaven."

She was transported along with three Catholic nuns under armed guard to a concentration camp in Yokohama. The four women were guarded by four police officers, one for each of them. After only two weeks, she was returned to her home in Shizuoka due to her frail health and placed under house arrest. She would remain there for the duration of the war.

Iki san was permitted to bring food to her once a week during the first year. But when Iki san and her husband lost their house in the bombing, they moved to his family's farm in the country and had difficulty finding food for themselves.

Lillie was held at the Shinjuku POW camp in Tokyo. When the soldiers came for her, she recognized one of them as one of her former students. He leaned toward her, as if to adjust her collar, and whispered in her ear, "Don't fight me, *Sensei*. I would have to hit you and I don't want to."

The children Lillie had been caring for and practically raising on her own were teenagers when Lillie was taken away. The eldest, Kimie, visited Lillie at the camp and found that she was not mistreated or tortured. The inmates provided for themselves, took care of the property, and did the washing for the soldiers who guarded them.

The scarcity of food everywhere in the country was the most difficult part of the war for those interned as well as the citizens of Japan.

HOUSE ARREST

The Japanese in the U.S. experienced similar circumstances. Those living on the West Coast in particular were removed from their homes and placed in relocation camps in Colorado, Arkansas, and other inland states. Hirosuke Ishiguro, the minister of the Westside Church of Christ who had assisted Sarah and others in Japan, was removed from his home. The FBI arrested him on March 13, 1942, and they questioned him extensively before transporting him to a civilian camp in Santa Fe, New Mexico. He was interned in several other detention centers before being released in October 1945. By the end of the war, many Japanese-Americans had nothing left to go back to. The Westside Church of Christ, the only Japanese-speaking congregation in the country, depended on help from their Christian brothers and sisters. Some entrusted treasured possessions to the care of their Christian family while they were in the relocation camps.

In Japan, however, the war exacted the greatest toll. Tokuo Mazawa had been converted in the Westside Church of Christ and educated at David Lipscomb College. He had been sent to Japan in 1935 to assist Sarah. He and his wife were living in Hiroshima when the first atomic bomb was dropped.

Sarah's house arrest was providential. Since she was occupying the property, those attempting to bring the church into the federation of churches were not able to confiscate it. Various schemes were tried in an effort to remove her from the house. At first, they tried to prove she was not sick so she could be returned to the concentration camp. When this failed, they tried to send her to a sanitarium, which again failed. When the United States began bombing Shizuoka, her opponents appealed to the government to evacuate her to the mountains for her safety. Their next attempt was to accuse her of an offense against the government in an attempt to send her to prison. Finally, they pronounced her insane and made arrangements to have her committed to an asylum in Manchuria. None of their efforts were successful, and she remained in her house.

Forced to live alone during the last two years of the war, she resorted to selling her furniture piece by piece in order to buy what little food was available. Since all property formerly owned by U.S. citizens was held by Japan's Finance Department, she had to go through much red tape in order to get permission to sell each item and then again to spend the money for the purchase of food. Even her garden was confiscated so she could not grow her own vegetables. In desperation, she said she "boiled leaves from trees for food, boiled and used water from cornstalks for sugar, used sea water for salt, and after months of meatless days I relished grasshoppers for meat, wishing I could have the same dish often."

"The loneliness, the starvation, the pressure, the tormentings could not have been endured but for the consciousness of God's presence and power," she recounted. "Indeed, to be left alone without God would be too awful for words, but to be left alone with God is a foretaste of heaven."

In the U.S., news from Japan was almost nonexistent, as normal channels of communication had been cut off. When McCaleb received word about Grace Farnham through the Swedish legation, he assumed the best for Lillie and Sarah as well. *Word and Work* optimistically reported in August 1942, "We think Sisters Andrews and Cypert will get along all right, though likely with some inconvenience."

The *Gospel Advocate* carried news of Lillie in a letter from McCaleb in April 1942. "Miss Lillie Cypert's sister in Porterville, Calif., has recently received a message from her, dated January 29, that she was at home carrying on her kindergarten work as usual. This indicates that Miss Sarah Andrews, of the city of Shizuoka, is permitted to do the same. Though their support has been cut off from the United States, I take it that they are being properly supported from funds I had to leave in Japan. That I was not permitted to bring this money out of Japan may have been providential."

McCaleb was referring to nearly six thousand dollars he left in the hands of Yunosuke Hiratsuka as he arranged for the care of his two churches before his departure. He appointed a committee of six men (three from the Zoshigaya church and three from the Kamitomizaka church) to take charge of the congregations. "All of our churches have determined to remain independent," he stated, meaning the churches under the direction of the a cappella Churches of Christ had refused to enter the

Kyodan. It wasn't until after the war that McCaleb learned all U.S. assets had been frozen and even the Japanese Christians were not able to use the money to help themselves or Lillie or Sarah.

Other Missionaries in the War

Missionaries in China did not escape persecution either. Ethel Mattley, a single woman in Hong Kong, was hospitalized shortly after the fall of the city, then placed in a camp until June 1942 when she was loaded on the *Asama Maru* to be sent to the United States. She reported that another missionary, Emmet L. Broaddus, died in Stanley Camp in Hong Kong from dysentery. In a letter to Don Carlos Janes, Mattley stated, "The woman in my cabin comes from Shizuoka (Japan) where Miss Andrews is and says she is well and doing fine, but chose to stay on. . . . Miss Cypert also remained behind."

In Lourenco Marques, Ethel Mattley was transferred to the *M.S. Gripsholm*, a Swedish ship that was used to exchange noncombatants (missionaries, diplomats, government workers, and civilians). Early in 1942, Britain and the United States proposed to the Japanese government an exchange of Japanese nationals who desired to be repatriated to Japan. Chartered by the U.S. government, the *Gripsholm* made a total of twelve round trips.

The *Gripsholm* left New York City on June 18, 1942, with 1,083 Japanese on board. After the exchange of passengers in Lourenco Marques, it returned to New York City on August 25 with 1,450 Americans. Ethel Mattley and Emily Cunningham, a missionary with the United Christian Missionary Society, were among those exchanged. It may have been Emily who sent a letter to *Word and Work* in November concerning Lillie. The *Word and Work* article stated:

> A missionary friend of Sister Cypert who came back on *The Gripsholm* has kindly written: "Miss Lillie Cypert was very anxious that I send you word of her as soon as we should land. She called at our house in June a few days before we sailed. She wishes me to tell you she is well and getting on as well

189

as can be expected. Food rationing is a difficult problem. In case all Americans are ordered to return on the next boat she will also probably return. Otherwise she seems in favor of remaining." Sister Cypert has cared for three Japanese children until they have become a part of her very self and she will not turn them loose to possible loss of their faith unless it becomes absolutely necessary. In this she shows a very great and worthy devotion.

With no mail exchanged between Japan and the U.S., news of those still in Japan was sparse and no money could be sent to them. The International Red Cross was able to set up a means of communication, but it was limited to one letter of twenty-five words every two months.

Another exchange of civilians took place in 1943. *Word and Work* informed their readers, "According to word from the Department of State, none of our group of missionaries in the Far East are being returned on this exchange ship except Sister Cypert who should reach the U.S. in early December. We are sorry for those who remain. . . ." Another note confirmed this information. "Sister Lillie D. Cypert is reported by the government as listed among the 1,250 American nationals now being repatriated from Japan and the Orient."

With no direct news of Sarah, the missionary journal continued to plead for prayers for her and others held in the bonds of the war. "Let us remember those missionaries who are still isolated in the Orient by the war. As they cannot correspond with us we do not know what difficulty they may have in getting food, what work, if any, they are able to do, and whether they are interned or free. Let us remember them in prayer *every day*." The *Word and Work*, although the journal of the independent, a cappella missionaries, also called for prayers for the "consecrated missionaries of the organ-using type in some of these fields."

LILLIE LEAVES JAPAN

Apparently ordered to leave Japan, Lillie boarded the *Teia Maru* in Yokohama and departed Japan on September 13, 1943. Conditions on board were described by some as "even worse than in the internment camp" since the ship was designed to accommodate 400 passengers and there were 1,500 North Americans on board, including Lillie and Grace Farnham. Each passenger was given a straw tick mattress six feet by twenty-four inches wide. The aisles between mattresses were just wide enough to walk through. Meals were taken in shifts and consisted of wormy rice and a small glass of water.

The ship took more than a month to reach the exchange point due to having to pass through mined waters without the aid of a minesweeper. They were transferred to the *M.S. Gripsholm* in Marmagoa, Portuguese India on October 19 over a period of three days. At one point, the entire exchange was halted because one of the Japanese passengers was missing. He had been lost overboard on the journey from New York, and the Japanese officials stopped the exchange. Finally an unknown American unselfishly volunteered to return to captivity, and the exchange resumed.

After everyone had transferred ships, one passenger recalled that the Christians got together and sang "In Christ there Is no East or West." The emaciated sojourners were treated to a Swedish smorgasbord that included cheese, ham, roast beef, turkey, vegetables, white bread with butter, and chocolate—foods they had not seen in years. On the afterdeck of the ship the American Red Cross handed out new clothing that had been donated by Americans. Finally, after four weeks on the *Teia Maru* and six weeks on the *M.S. Gripsholm*, on December 1, 1943, the ship sailed up New York harbor, past the Statue of Liberty.

Once back on U.S. soil, Lillie phoned her brother Creighton to ask for money to be able to travel to his home in Oklahoma. Lillie's sister Sadie provided more funds for Lillie to go from Oklahoma to California where Sadie lived. Janes appealed to the brotherhood on her behalf saying, "She has had 26 hard years in a climate that is difficult for Americans and has come with next to nothing, but friends are responding and should continue to give as long as there is need. A point of honor is involved in this matter." Visits with her family had to wait a few weeks as Lillie underwent medical treatment in Louisville. She was seen by "the eye man, doctors, the dentist and X-ray laboratory." With new glasses and a lot of dental work, she headed off to see her family after a short visit with Sarah's mother to bring what little news she had of her fellow missionary.

Lillie did not return to Japan. She did assist as an interpreter in a Japanese relocation camp in Arkansas for a time during the remaining years of the war. Her deep affection for the Japanese people and involvement with them caused some concern among those at the U.S. Department of State. It is reported that she was kept under surveillance by the FBI and questioned several times. The Kichijoji church building, and Lillie's home, escaped destruction from the U.S. bombing raids, but it was torn down following the war.

Lillie eventually moved to Los Angeles and lived with Michio and Lorraine Nagai for about a year. Lillie had known Lorraine in Zoshigaya when Lorraine had worked briefly for McCaleb in 1938. Unmarried at that time, Lorraine Hasegawa had grown up in California but attended a girls' high school in Tokyo. She knew both English and Japanese and was supported by the Cornell Avenue Church of Christ in Santa Rosa. Michio and Lorraine met while students at Abilene Christian College and were married in 1946. The Nagai family was actively engaged with the Westside Church of Christ in Los Angeles, as was Lillie, and the congregation purchased a mobile home for Lillie to live in behind the church building.

The three Yanai children Lillie had to leave behind in Japan continued to live in her heart. When the war ended she managed to locate them with the help of Harry Robert Fox Jr. and sent "care packages" to them. She arranged for a scholarship for the youngest boy, Steve, to attend Pepperdine College in 1949 and even paid for his ship passage to Los Angeles.

When Lillie fell and broke her hip in 1950, she had to move to her sister's home in Porterville, California, to be cared for. Apparently, she had a major stroke while there. Her obituary in the *Gospel Advocate* provided some details. "Sister Lillie Cypert passed from this life during the night of August 13, 1954. She died in her sleep. A heartfelt thanks is extended to all who so generously contributed to her care during her prolonged illness. She had been completely paralyzed for some time. The kindness of many who consistently gave her support made it possible for us to give her the best care during her last days." She was buried in the Vandalia Cemetery in Porterville.

Her legacy continues in Japan in the students she taught in her kindergarten. Ikuko Maejima, one of her students, still lives across the street from the school and every year five of Lillie's graduates meet for a reunion in honor of their teacher.

HETTIE LEE AFTER THE WAR

Hettie Lee's activities during and after the war involved several locations and jobs. After updating her teaching certificate in Hawaii and docking in Los Angeles, she took a position as a clerk-typist for the government in Texas. Passing a civil service exam, she was assigned to a desk in San Antonio, where she was working when Pearl Harbor was bombed. During the war, she worked in Washington, D.C., and in a relocation center in Arkansas helping the displaced Japanese. It wasn't until July 1947 that she was allowed to return to Japan, where she continued to assist the churches in their work for two years. She went again in 1952, staying until 1965, teaching part of that time in the International School. She made two more brief visits to Japan before retiring to the Christian Care Center in Mesquite, Texas. She passed away September 18, 1986, shortly before her ninetieth birthday, and she is buried in Crown Hill Cemetery in Dallas.

CHAPTER NINETEEN

SARAH: ALONE WITH GOD

Sarah Andrews did not fair as well as her companions during the war. Shizuoka was a small city with a population of about thirty-five thousand but it contained valuable war plants, arsenals, and the Mitsubishi Aircraft Engine factory. From her home, Sarah observed several B-29 air raids on the outskirts of her city and one neighboring town. On the night of June 19, 1945, her section of the city was targeted. Thirty planes deposited over 189 tons of incendiary bombs on the city. It was estimated that 66 percent of the city's built up area was consumed in the fire. Air raid shelters consisted of a shallow hole in the ground next to one's house with a wooden roof covered with soil and clay. The night of June 19, over two thousand died and more than twelve thousand were injured. The unclaimed bodies lay for three days along the river until they were cremated.

Two planes from the 314th Bomber Wing collided over the city and came crashing down in a field west of the city. Twenty-three U.S. airmen perished in the collision. The next morning a local businessman, Fukumatsu Itoh, went to the crash site and found a dented canteen belonging to one of the airmen. Itoh san mourned for both the Japanese and American dead and erected a wooden cross for the Americans. Later, he became a Buddhist monk and erected two monuments in memory of those who died that night. Each June, according to a report about that bombing raid, there is a memorial service at the monuments for the war dead. It has become a custom to pour some bourbon from the original canteen on the American headstone.

Incredibly, not only did Sarah survive the attack, but she also slept through the entire bombing raid that night even though bombs had been dropped and houses burned within sixty feet of her home. She awoke the next morning feeling more refreshed than she had in months. It was only when she looked outside and saw the destruction of everything around her, including the temple across the street, that she became aware of what had taken place. Had she awoke and attempted to flee, she probably would have been killed by the bombs or mobbed by angry Japanese. Although the U.S. military had dropped pamphlets prior to the attack warning civilians to flee, the local authorities had not allowed the populace to read them.

The morning after the attack, seventeen injured civilians were brought to Sarah's house, and she was ordered to care for them. In a state of exhaustion and near starvation, within a few days she could no longer stand and had to crawl from person to person to care for them. After two weeks, the patients were moved out leaving behind an infestation of fleas.

About two months later, around the middle of August, Sarah noticed the B-29s were no longer flying overhead. Soon, the woman who brought her daily allotment of food informed her that the war had ended, that Emperor Hirohito "in sympathy for his people had graciously delivered them."

By the first of September, evidence of peace was seen as foxholes were filled, food was delivered by the government, Christians were free to visit, and church services resumed. On Sunday morning, October 28 an American GI, William Billingsley, drove across the mountains from Yokohama in a jeep with a fellow soldier and an interpreter in an attempt to find Sarah. Sarah's sister Myrtle Thompson, lived near an airbase in Tyler, Texas. Myrtle's husband, T. B. Thompson, was the preacher for the Tyler Church of Christ. Each Sunday, Myrtle invited some young soldiers home for dinner and told them about Sarah. She gave each of them a card with Sarah's last known address and asked them, if they were shipped to the Pacific, to look for her. Her family had had no word from Sarah for over two years and was unaware if she was alive or dead.

However it was an overheard conversation at the Tyler Church of Christ that resulted in Billingsley's search for Sarah. Sarah's sister heard William Billingsley's wife mention that her husband had been sent to Japan with the occupation forces. Myrtle asked for Billingsley's address and wrote to him, pleading for him to attempt to find Sarah, whose home was located between two occupation zones. Sarah was just returning home that morning in October from worship at the church about ten miles away when the jeep pulled up.

When Billingsley saw Sarah, who weighed only seventy-five pounds at that point, he asked if she was Sarah Andrews. "Why, yes," she replied. "But how did you know I was here?" The GI's left their rations with Sarah, as the only food she had left at that time was five walnuts. Billingsley returned four days later with a jeep loaded with food, warm clothing, and fuel to get her through the winter. Her home soon became the distribution point for goods to be shared with her Japanese friends. A lady and her daughter came to live with Sarah and helped with the daily chores.

Billingsley was able to give Sarah letters from her family, whom she had not heard from in years. During the four years of the war, Sarah had received only three twenty-five-word letters—two from her mother and one from a lady at the Walnut Street Church—and those had come through the Red Cross during the first year of war. For nearly three years, she received no word from home and had not heard anyone speak English. Communication continued to be slow. She was able to send letters through the army chaplain, but it took about twenty days to send and receive one letter.

She was allowed to travel to Tokyo on the army trains for free as "Recovered Personnel." She spent several days in the hospital in Tokyo for a check up that was a double treat—she received medical care as well as a comfortable place to stay when hotels were filled to capacity. She enjoyed the "nice American army food" and gained some weight. However, the doctors determined her heart was not very strong and recommended against making the trip to the States at that time.

When the Japanese saw how well she was being treated, one commented, "Surely the Supreme Being is with that woman!" Sarah said, "To have these people recognize God and ascribe unto him the power for my deliverance made me rejoice that I had been counted worthy to suffer." It also pleased her that because she stayed, none of her churches or their property had passed into the hands of the federation of churches.

Unable to return to the States immediately due to her deteriorated health condition, she spent Thanksgiving in the company of the Occupation Army in Shizuoka. She told the chaplain that day that she was especially thankful for "my citizenship in heaven and on earth." It wasn't until after her congregations were assured of being allowed to continue as independent churches without government interference that Sarah began to think of continuing her work in Japan when she was well.

Sarah Comes Home

When doctors declared her strong enough to be sent back home, she began planning her return. "I am hoping to resume my bit of service . . . after my visit home," she told her friends in Japan.

A high-ranking Japanese official spoke of Sarah in a letter of commendation. "Throughout the 30 years that she has been here, her career has been wholly devoted to social work, such as the preaching of the gospel, managing of kindergarten, relief of the sick and helpless. She has often suffered insufficient funds for her work and went home to America three times to raise the necessary funds, while she herself has been living in contented poverty, which fact is making a deep impression upon people about her."

Others noted her humility and "down-to-earth good sense," as fellow missionary Harry Robert Fox Jr. put it. He admired her determination to fight against materialism, selfishness, and ostentation.

The religious laws were revoked and the church was able to enjoy freedom again. Sarah wrote to her supporters that "the victory of God's will as regards the church in Japan is the source of greatest joy and thanksgiving. There is hope for the future. Christians are not without vision and the people in their dilemma are seeking the truth."

Sarah left her three surviving congregations in the hands of the Japanese Christians and came back to the U.S. aboard the *U.S.S. Ainsworth* in July 1946 for medical treatment. She had been receiving some medical care in the hospital in Tokyo, as she was required to be declared fit for travel before she was allowed to sail for home.

Once back in the States, she was given more advanced medical attention including some vision care and dental work. All of her teeth had to be removed and a full set of dentures made for her because her own teeth had deteriorated so badly. She reported having a tremor in her hand so severe that she could not write legibly, but she made do with a portable Remington typewriter for her correspondence. Her heart had also been weakened by the years of malnutrition and near starvation although her weight soared to nearly one hundred pounds after a few months back home. Many were surprised at her decision to resume the work in Japan. "It takes a lean horse to run a good race," she informed them.

While recuperating, she began again to replace the study notes of Galatians and Ephesians that had been destroyed twice during the war—confiscated by soldiers once and bombed the second time. She also resumed writing a history of the church in Japan, a task she had begun while under house arrest but was too weak to finish at that time. Although her health would never be completely restored, she carried no resentment concerning her experience. "Now that the curtain has been lifted," she wrote, "I am forgetting trials and am glad that I can. I want to remember the lessons learned and profit by them."

Early in 1947, she wrote to McCaleb, who was living and working in California, that she hoped to return to Japan in early 1948 if a passport could be obtained. "God willing, I hope to return," she said. "The call comes ringing. The three churches where I labored are waiting."

She had planned to spend Christmas of 1947 with her mother and sister in Texas but was unable to make the trip. She celebrated the holidays with the McCalebs in California instead.

Sarah remained in Los Angeles through early April when news came that her mother, living in Florida with one of Sarah's sisters, had passed away. Sarah went to Dickson for the funeral and then spent the summer with her sister in Florida. Although family and friends tried to convince her to stay, her heart was in Japan. "That is my work and my people. I can do more there on a cot than here on my feet," she declared.

She was even more eager to return after receiving news that there were 120 children in attendance at Bible study on Sunday, March 28, at the Shizuoka church. She was intent on finishing the study outlines so that they would be able to understand the Bible without her to teach them. Her correspondent informed her that "a prayer for my speedy return is offered each Lord's day."

Her financial support had been virtually nonexistent during the war years when her friends and family were not even sure she was alive. When she began to make preparations in 1947 to return to Japan, she had to begin seeking funds all over again. This time I. B. Bradley, who had faithfully solicited and forwarded all of her funds prior to the war, asked to be relieved of the responsibility due to his age and health. Instead, the church in Dickson would continue to be her sponsoring church and send all contributions to her through their treasury.

Her plans for the work in Japan included building a rest home to care for the widows, orphans, and convalescents the war had caused. She dreamed of a large home with land for trees and gardens and livestock. Later that summer, she visited friends in Tennessee and may have been at Walnut Street Church when it celebrated Homecoming Day that fall. She passed the winter in Texas with relatives before continuing on to Los Angeles.

SARAH'S FINAL TRIP TO JAPAN

Once her medical and dental needs were taken care of, and a passport secured, Sarah took the train from Los Angeles to San Francisco, arriving in the Bay City on April 28, 1949. From there she sailed on the *S.S. Scud* to Seattle, arriving two days later. She spent two days with a Sister Hamilton who kept a spare room available for traveling missionaries, and at midnight on May 3, Sarah left on the *S.S. Scud* for Japan. She was one of only six passengers on board since the ship was a freighter rather than a passenger ship. She was able to save eighty dollars by traveling in this manner—money she intended to use for her new building project.

Since it was less nauseating to be on the deck of the rocky boat, she spent most of the voyage topside where she made the acquaintance of a Buddhist lady who was fearful of the ocean waves. Sarah offered her reassurance of God's watchful care for them. Sarah was met in Yokohama on May 20 by a group of fourteen friends waving from the pier. Her return made news in several Japanese papers.

Only four churches of those originally established by the Restoration Movement missionaries survived after the war. Three of them were ones Sarah had begun— Okitsu, Shimizu and Shizuoka. When she returned to Japan, she began a fourth congregation in Numazu. McCaleb's congregations at Zoshigaya and Kamitomizaka merged during the war. This congregation joined the Kyodan in 1944, while a remnant formed the Tokyo Central Church in 1946 (today known as the Ochanomizu Church). The Ota church in Ibaraki, started by the Moreheads, reopened shortly after the war.

Although beset by constant health problems (pneumonia, migraine headaches, chronic colitis, prolapsed intestines, and continued weight loss back down to eighty pounds), she saw her dream become reality. With her help, the church in Numazu erected a new building in 1953 large enough to include a church meeting room downstairs and living quarters for her upstairs in addition to some extra rooms in which older members of the church could live. Typical of her modest lifestyle, she said after the building was done that it was larger and more luxurious than she had anticipated, and she felt embarrassed to be living in it.

She made one more trip home, not even returning for her brother Pete's funeral in 1950. Medical reasons were the only thing that could bring her back to the States. She needed to be fitted for a special girdle to cope with the prolapsed intestines, so she crossed the Pacific once more in 1956. She left the United States for the last time on July 12, 1958, arriving back in Yokohama two weeks later in spite of a typhoon at sea. She wrote friends after arriving that she stayed in bed and had a good rest during the storm, "leaving the termination of the storm with God."

She continued teaching Bible classes as long as her health permitted and even enjoyed a three-day vacation on the Idzu Peninsula in 1960. Missionary Elmer Prout recalled a visit from her at his mission point in Ibaraki around that time. "She was increasingly frail in body," he remembered, "but strong and radiant in spirit. Sustained by her convictions founded in the faith of the Lord Christ." During Prout's mid-week Bible study the song leader asked Sarah for her favorite song. Without hesitation she replied, "Peace, Perfect Peace." Prout concluded that it was the assurance that "the blood of Jesus whispers peace within" that had sustained her through the war years.

The summer heat, hardening of her arteries, and low blood pressure contributed to a series of strokes in the summer of 1961. Hettie Lee, back in Japan at the time, recalled how the Japanese Christians flocked to see what they could do for her. They came to see her daily, bringing food and flowers. Men and women took turns sitting up with her at night in shifts. After a week of weakness and difficulty speaking, Hettie Lee and Iki san took her to the hospital in Tokyo on July 21. When informed two weeks later that there was nothing more the hospital could do for her, Iki san brought her back to her home in Numazu where she had a second stroke that proved fatal. She passed away on September 16, 1961.

Through an oversight in communications, her brothers and sisters learned of her death when a reporter phoned to inquire about funeral arrangements. By the time they could learn the details, Sarah's body had already been cremated. A memorial service was conducted in a large rented hall in order to accommodate the hundreds who desired to pay their respects. Part of the service included a tape-recorded message in Japanese that Sarah had made a few weeks before her death as a means of comforting those who would grieve her passing.

According to her wishes, her ashes were buried in Japan. Japanese Christians erected a large monument at her gravesite that reads in part, "She dedicated her whole life to her beloved Japan and Japanese people. She taught and trained many believers in Jesus Christ and gave all to the glory to God. When she knew it was her time to leave, she recited Psalm 103 for hours, which moved those attending her deathbed to tears." The monument includes the first two verses of that psalm: "Praise the Lord, O my soul; all my inmost being, praise his holy name. Praise the Lord, O my soul, and forget not all his benefits. . . ."

One of her nephews, Mack Wayne Craig, recalled his Aunt Sarah telling how many times she had given away all of the food and money she had to help those around her. He was "appalled at the idea of her giving until she had absolutely nothing left for herself." When he asked her if she wasn't afraid of starving, she replied, "Honey, there has never been a time when I have given away everything I had that the next boat from America didn't bring food or money or both."

Her devoted companion Iki san survived the war with her husband in their country home. Iki san maintained contact with Sarah's family and wrote of a memorial service held in 1981, twenty years after Sarah's death. It was attended by more than one hundred people who came to remember and honor Sarah. Iki san and her husband were among the number and reported that the churches Sarah started were still meeting and growing.

The paths that these single women blazed during the first half of the twentieth century inspired numerous other women to go to various places around the world in the years since. The decision to leave their comfortable homes, the companionship of friends, the security of family, and the modern conveniences of the West to go to a country where the traditions, language, housing, food, clothing, and religion were all so foreign was not an easy decision to make. As one considers the results of the choices made by these dedicated young women, McCaleb's words seem fitting:

> To the young, especially, I would say, Look well to your decisions, for on them depends not only your own future destiny, but that of others.

APPENDIX:
BIOGRAPHICAL DATA

Andrews, Sarah Shepherd (d/o Will Andrews and Adele Shepherd)
b. 26 Nov. 1892 Dickson, Tenn.
d. 16 Sept. 1961 Numazu, Japan   bur. Numazu, Japan
Japan 1916–1961

Armbruster, Rose Theresa (d/o Alphonse Armbruster and Lena Danehart)
b. 24 Jan. 1875 Springfield, Ill.
d. 15 July 1950 Camarillo St. Hosp., Ventura, Calif.
Japan 1903–1932

Asbury, Jessie Joanna (d/o H. B. Asbury and T. B. Hitch)
b. 16 March 1877 Germantown, Augusta Co., Ky.
d. 9 Sept. 1947 Los Angeles, Calif.
Japan 1901–1932

Beach, Emma (d/o Joel Beach and Lilly)
b. 19 April 1891 Mayesville, S.C.
Japan 1930–1934

Brown, Winifred May (d/o J. W. Brown and Tina)
b. Nov. 1889 Tex.
m. William Powell Lee @ 1920
b. 11 Nov. 1890 Tex. (s/o J. S. Lee and Jane)
d. 1939
Japan 1913–1918

Clawson, Bertha Fidelia (d/o Asa Clawson and Rebecca Hoover)
b. 21 Dec. 1868 Strawn, Coffee Co., Kans.
d. 6 Feb. 1957 San Gabriel, Calif.   bur. Forest Lawn Cem., Los Angeles, Calif.
Japan 1898–1931; 1935–1937

Craynon, Nettie (d/o Thomas Craynon and Martha)
b. 18 July 1878 Ky.
Japan 1896–1897

Crosno, Clara May (d/o George Crosno and Ollie Neeley)
b. 4 Dec. 1893 Duncan, Okla.
d. June 1977 Cheyenne, Laramie Co., Wyo.
m. Joseph Ahlstrom 1932
Japan 1921–1922

(Cunningham) Sturgeon, Doris Elaine (d/o William D. Cunningham and Emily Boyd)
b. 29 Aug. 1902 Karuizawa, Japan

m. Leo Dallas Sturgeon
   b. 19 July 1896 Chicago, IL
Japan 1927–1929

Cunningham, Emily Blackstone Boyd
   b. 22 Feb. 1873 Oil City, Pa.
   d. 25 Dec. 1953   bur. Zoshigaya Cem., Tokyo, Japan
   m. William Dayton Cunningham, June 1898
      b. 19 July 1864 Dawson, Pa.
      d. 24 June 1936 Rochester, Minn.
Japan 1937–1942 (widowed)

Cypert, Lillie Delenzia (d/o Eli Newton Cypert and Euphamia Cable)
   b. 27 May 1890 Oak Flat, Red River Tnshp, Searcy Co., Ark.
   d. 13 Aug. 1954 Porterville, Tulare Co., Calif.   bur. Vandalia Cem., Porterville,
      Tulare Co., Calif.
Japan 1917–1943

Douglas, Bertha Colera (d/o James Douglas and Sarah Todd)
   b. 8 April 1889 St. Claire, Cedar Co., Mo.
   d. 23 Nov. 1950 Santa Cruz, Calif.
Japan 1920–1925

Draper, Alice Olin (d/o Dr. William H. Draper and Ruth Dana)
   b. 23 March 1883 N.Y.
   m. Edward Clark Carver 5 Sept. 1908 Islesboro, Maine
Japan @1900–1907

Ewing, Hettie Lee (d/o Marcus Ewing and Lenora Lily Stringer)
   b. 11 Oct. 1896 Cleburne, Johnson Co., Tex.
   d. 18 Sept. 1986 Tex.   bur. Crown Hill Cem., Dallas, Tex.
Japan 1926–1940; 1947–1949; 1952–1964; 1966–1967; 1968–1972

Farnham, Ella Grace (d/o Joseph Farnham and Ella)
   b. 31 July 1890 Idaho
   d. 25 May 1984 Marion Co., Ore.
Japan 1925–1943; 1947–1960

Garst, Gretchen Hazel (d/o Charles Garst and Laura DeLany)
   b. 1 April 1887 Akita, Japan
   d. 25 April 1952   bur. Glendale Cem., Polk Co., Iowa
Japan 1912–1925

Gibson, Martha Ellis (d/o George Gibson)
   b. 27 Jan. 1897 St. Louis, Mo.
   d. Jan. 1983 Columbia, Boone Co., Mo.
Japan 1924–1932

(Gilbert) Briscoe, Lena (Lean?) (d/o Walter Gilbert and Mollie)
   b. 24 April 1896 Vernon, Tex.

d. 10 April 1979 Potter, Tex.

m. Jerry Bowler Briscoe 8 Nov. 1925 Deaf Smith, Tex.

    b. 26 July 1877 Ralls, Mo.

Japan 1923–1924

(Goodrich) Kelly, Carrie (d/o Orren Goodrich and Joanna Tucker)

    b. 12 July 1871 Oskaloosa, Ohio

    d. 17 Dec. 1901 Changteh, Hunon, China   bur. Changteh, Hunon, China

    m. Dr. William D. Kelly 22 Aug. 1900 Shanghai, China

        b. 1 Aug. 1874 St. Paul, Minn.

        d. 22 June 1957 Peking, China

        he mar. 2nd Grace Hill

Japan 1899–1900

(Hagin) Rumfalo, Edith Genieveve (d/o Fred Hagin and Myrtle Willett)

    b. 13 Jan. 1893 Greeley, Delaware Co., Iowa

    d. 29 Sept. 1968 Bellflower, Orange Co., Calif.   bur. Rose Hills Memorial Park Cem., Los Angeles Co, Calif.

    m. John D. Francis 25 Dec. 1928 Calif.

        b. 7 April 1889 Maui, Hawaii (s/o Manoel deFranca Campainha and Antoinetta)

        d. 25 Jan. 1949 Modesto, Calif.   bur. Rose Hills Memorial Park Cem., Los Angeles Co., Calif.

    2nd Anthony Rumfalo

Japan 1919–1924

Harding, Cecile Elizabeth (d/o James Robert Harding and Carrie Verona Leonard)

    b. 23 Aug. 1885 Tyro, Kans.

    d. 24 Nov. 1928 Spokane, Wash.   bur. Garfield Cem., Whitman Co., Wash.

Japan 1925–1928

Harker, Hazel Florence (d/o Samuel Harker and Margaret)

    b. 11 May 1887 Albany, Ind.

    d. 24 Nov. 1963 Ind.

Japan 1923–1925

Harrison, Calla James (d/o Julia Harrison Wehr)

    b. 28 Sept. 1859 N. Madison, Ind.

    d. 5 July 1937 Honolulu, Hawaii   bur. Honolulu, Hawaii

Japan 1886–1897

Hiatt, Jennie May

    b. 26 May 1886 Ill.

    d. May 1969 Eureka, Woodford Co., Ill.

Japan 1908–@1929

(Hostetter) Smyser, Atta Carme (d/o Hiram Hostetter and Miss Walker)

    b. 6 Feb. 1869 Minerva, Ohio

    d. 16 July 1945 Claremont, Los Angeles Co., Calif.; bur. Oak Park Cem., Claremont, Calif.

m. Martin Mosser Smyser 13 May 1905
 b. 19 Jan. 1875 Lisburn, Pa. (s/o Henry Smyser and Catherine Shetter)
 d. 24 March 1955 Yokote, Akita Ken, Japan bur. Akita, Japan
 he m. 2nd Ethel Nellie Hoag
Japan 1892–1905

Johnson, Kate V. (d/o Elizabeth)
 b. 5 Nov. 1860 St. Louis, Mo.
 d. 29 Jan. 1919 Madison, Ind. bur. Madison, Jefferson Co., Ind.
Japan June 1886–1917

(Johnson) Calderwood, Rose Ruetta (d/o J. W. Johnson)
 b. 18 Dec. 1878 Cuterville, Walnut City, Appanoose Co., Iowa
 d. 1 Oct. 1957
 m. Jesse S. Calderwood 1918
  b. May 1875 Wellsburg, Brooke Co., W.Va. (s/o David Calderwood and Laura Frazier)
  d. 22 July 1949
Japan 1906–1912

Jones, Christine C. (d/o Albert Jones and Clara)
 b. @ Dec. 1907 Temple Hill, Barren Co., Ky.
 d. May 1979 Hickman, Fulton Co., Ky.
Japan 1931–1932

Jones, Ethel L.
 b. @1918 Tex.
 d. 17 Oct. 1964 Newark, Ohio bur. Granville, Ohio
Japan 1934–1939

Kennedy, Clara E. (d/o James Kennedy and Edith)
 b. 26 Dec. 1901 Portland, Cumberland Co., Maine
Japan 1924–1936

Lankford, Edith Marie (d/o Levi Lankford and Callie)
 b. 14 March 1908 Hohenwald, Lewis Co., Tenn.
 d. July 1949 Latham, Logan Co., Ill.
Japan 1928–1929

(Lediard) Doan, Mary Frances (d/o James Lediard and Jane Eliza Baldwin)
 b. 24 Oct. 1881 Hillsburg, Ontario, Canada
 d. 13 May 1959
 m. Robert Austin Doan 15 Sept. 1923 Kobe, Japan
  b. 1874
  d 18 March 1936 Westerville, Franklin Co., Ohio
Japan 1906–1923 (single); 1937–1939 (widowed)

Lehman, Lois Alberta (d/o Joel B. Lehman and Ethia)
 b. 8 July 1897 Edwards, Miss.

d. 15 Dec. 1977 Los Angeles, Calif.
Japan 1922–1927

Lemmon, Vivian Mae (d/o William Sherman Lemmon and Anna Beardsley)
b. 27 July 1902 Norwalk, Warren Co., Iowa
d. 26 Aug. 1987 Tanabe, Japan   cremated in Japan
Japan 1930–1936; 1952–1987

(Lewis) Young, Stella Walker (d/o Thompson Walker and Sallie Lyon)
b. 17 Dec. 1882 Lincoln, Turnersville, Ky.
d. 7 July 1969 Selma, Dallas Co., Ala.
m. Thomas A. Young @1911(s/o Thomas Younghusband and Mary Ann Crawford)
b. 7 Feb. 1882 Alleghany, Pa.
d. 24 Feb. 1949 Selma, Dallas Co., Ala.
Japan 1905–1911

(Lusby) Kelley, Majel (d/o James Lusby and Emma Threlkeld)
b. 2 Jan. 1907 Grayson, Ky.
d. 13 Aug. 1986 Atlanta, Ga.   bur. Grayson, Ky.
m. Ray "Skinny" Kelley 8 Sept. 1933 Grayson, Ky.
b. 3 March 1903 Pa. (s/o Charles Kelley and Virginia Russ)
d. 10 May 1976 Pa. bur. Schuylkill Haven, Pa.
Japan 1928–1931

(Lyons) Ritchie, Iris N. (d/o Fernando Lyons and Laura Brown)
b. 3 June 1891 Mo.
d. Oct 1970 Palo Alto, Santa Clara Co., Calif.
m. George Lawrence Ritchie @1924
b. 8 May 1882 Ill. (s/o George Ritchie and Mabel Hicks)
d. 13 May 1967 Sacramento, Calif.
Japan 1914–1915

(Madden) Braley, Grace Emma (d/o Milton B. Madden and Maude Whitmore)
b. 13 March 1910 Topeka, Kans.
d. 23 Feb. 1990 Sun City, Ariz.
m. Gerald Neal Braley 11 Feb. 1939
Japan 1919–1936

Miller, Alice (d/o James Q. Miller and Susan Ragland)
b. 30 Jan.1853 Cadiz, Trigg Co., Ky.
d. 5 March 1928 Zoshigaya, Japan   bur. Zoshigaya Cem., Tokyo, Japan
Japan 1895–1928

Oldham, Lavinia (d/o Thompson Oldham and Nancy Phelps)
b. 28 Jan. 1856 Mt. Sterling, Montgomery Co., Ky.
d. 26 June 1927 Lexington, Fayette Co., Ky.   bur. Mt. Sterling, Montgomery Co., Ky.
Japan 1892–1921

Palmer, Jewel Irene
    b. 19 Aug. 1894 Columbia, Macon Co., Mo.
    d. 21 March 1949 Enid, Garfield Co., Okla.
    Japan 1918–1929

Parker, Edith (d/o William Parker and Georgeanna)
    b. 2 May 1878 Palmyra, Emerson Co., Mo.
    d. 13 Jan. 1923 Kobe, Japan
    Japan 1909–1923

Penrod, Christine T. (d/o Joseph Penrod and Louisa)
    b. 24 Jan. 1864 Crawfordsville, Ind.
    d. 1922   bur. Zoshigaya Reienn Foreign Cemetery, Japan
    Japan @1897–1920

Remington, Dr. Gertrude (d/o Frank Remington and Ann)
    b. 1866
    d. 24 Nov. 1907 Thomasville, Ga.
    Japan 1904–1906

Richey, Helen Lenore (d/o Horace Richey and Martha)
    b. 21 Nov. 1891 Cincinnati, Hamilton Co., Ohio
    d. 4 Sept. 1941 Columbus, Franklin Co., Ohio
    Japan 1921–1932

(Rioch) Miller, Mary McKenzie
    b. @ 1873 Hamilton, Ontario, Canada
    d. 10 Dec. 1957
    m. George Miller 1915
        d. <1949
    Japan 1892–1915

(Robison) Crewdson, Amy Jean (d/o Dr. Henry Barton Robison and Dora Sledd)
    b. 20 Oct. 1896 Lexington, Ky.
    d. 11 Aug. 1987 Driftwood, Hays Co., Tex.
    m. Hubert Cecil Sarvis, March 1924 Osaka, Japan
        d. 30 Sept. 1931
    2nd Ira Dorwin Crewdson 24 July 1970 Houston, Tex.
        b. 19 Feb 1893 Woodbine, Harrison Co., Iowa (s/o George Crewdson and
            Barbara Watts)
        d. 15 Jan. 1975 Caldwell, Canyon Co., Idaho; bur. Little Rock, Pulaski Co., Ark.
    Japan 1920–1924 (single); 1931–1935 (widowed)

Schoonover, Ruth Marie (d/o Louis Schoonover and Celia)
    b. 8 April 1898 Ft. Wayne, Ind.
    d. 26 Nov. 1948 Tanabe, Japan   bur. Mabashi, Tokyo, Japan
    Japan 1931–1941; 1948

Scott, Ada Calista (d/o Dr. Elisha Challen Scott and Josepha Dunshee)
    b. 14 Oct. 1886 Iowa City, Iowa
    d. 9 Oct 1946 Des Moines, Iowa   bur. Woodland Cem., Des Moines, Polk Co., Iowa
    Japan 1916–1925

Scott, Lucia M. (d/o Porter Scott and Lucy Palmer)
    b. 14 Oct. 1869 Chester, Geauga Co., Ohio
    d. 26 June 1926 Calif.
    Japan 1892–1897

Shimmel, Edith (d/o James Shimmel and Anna Finland)
    b. May 1881
    Japan 1934–1939

Trout, Jessie Mary (d/o Archibald E. Trout and Catherine Donald)
    b. 26 July 1895 Owen Sound, Ontario, Canada
    d. 1990
    Japan 1921–1933; 1935–1940

Ward, Isabelle Mae (d/o Mr. Ward and Miss Hutchinson)
    b. 24 May 1875 Wilmington, Ill.
    d. 10 May 1959 Los Angeles, Calif.
    Japan @1902–1919

Wirick, Loduska J. (d/o Joseph Wirick and Sarah Meyers)
    b. 8 June 1858 Cedar Co., Iowa
    d. 30 April 1914 Tokyo, Japan   bur. Somei Cem., Toshima-ku, Japan
    Japan 1890–1914

Wright, Edith Elnora (d/o Fred O. Wright and Lucy Cook)
    b. 26 Sept. 1873 Chelsea, Mass.
    d. 21 March 1938 Los Angeles, Calif.
    m. --- Pettijohn <1906
    Japan 1902–1903

Yoho, Virginia Dee (d/o Jefferson Wylie Yoho and Elva Alma Wayman)
    b. 27 Jan. 1903 Bethany, W.Va.
    d. 9 Jan. 1976 Indianapolis, Ind.
    m. Lt. Col. Allan Ellsworth Eldridge, 21 Jan. 1946
        b. 21 May 1900 Hartford, Conn. (s/o Hiram Eldridge)
        d. Aug. 1985
    Japan 1930–1933

BIBLIOGRAPHY

Books

Berry, Minta Sue. "Sarah Andrews: Eyes on the Risen Son." Unpublished Manuscript, 2002.

Boyd, R. Vernon. "A History of the Stone–Campbell Churches in Michigan." Unpublished Manuscript, n.d.

Burney, Norma, Paul Pratt, Bill Turner and Betty Turner, eds. *Japan Missions 1984: 100th Anniversary Edition*. Tokyo, Japan: New Life League, 1984.

Butchart, Reuben. *The Disciples of Christ in Canada Since 1830*. Toronto: Canadian Headquarters Publications, 1949.

Daggett, Shawn. "History of Christian Missions." D.Min. diss., Harding University Graduate School of Religion, 2007.

Ewing, Hettie Lee. *She Hath Done What She Could*. Ed. Orlan Sawey and Nina Sawey. Dallas: Gospel Teachers Pub., 1974.

———. *Another Look at Japan*. Dallas: Temple Publishing Co., 1977.

Filbeck, David. *The First Fifty Years: A Brief History of the Direct-Support Missionary Movement*. Joplin, Mo.: College Press Pub. Co., 1980.

Foster, Douglas A., Paul M. Blowers, Anthony L. Dunnavant, and D. Newell Williams, eds. *The Encyclopedia of the Stone–Campbell Movement*. Grand Rapids: Eerdmans, 2004.

Garst, Laura DeLany. *A West-Pointer in the Land of the Mikado*. London: Fleming H. Revell, 1913.

Ion, A. Hamish. *The Cross and the Rising Sun: The British Protestant Missionary Movement in Japan, Korea, and Taiwan 1865–1945*. Ontario: Wilfred Laurier University Press, 1992.

Janes, Don Carlos. *Our World Tour*. Chicago: W.B. Conkey Co., 1924.

———. *Missionary Biographies*. Louisville: Janes Printing Co., 1940.

McCaleb, James Moody. *Christ the Light of the World*. Nashville: McQuiddy Printing Co., 1911.

———. *On the Trail of the Missionaries*. Nashville: Gospel Advocate Co., 1930.

———. *Once Traveled Roads*. Nashville: Gospel Advocate Co., 1934.

McCoy, Rollin Delos. *Japan and the Japan Mission*. Cincinnati: Foreign Christian Missionary Society, n.d.

McLean, Archibald. *Missionary Addresses*. St. Louis: Christian Publishing Co., 1895.

———. *A Circuit of the Globe*. St. Louis: Christian Publishing Co., 1899.

———. *The History of the Foreign Christian Missionary Society*. London: Fleming H. Revell, 1919.

Nixon, Brenda. "Lillie's Story." Unpublished Manuscript, 2006.

Philpott, Elaine Wolfe. *Inez Scott Cartwright: Her Life and Ministry*, Nashville: Disciples of Christ Historical Society, 1999.

Schug, Howard and Jesse P. Sewell. *The Harvest Field*. Athens, Ala.: Bible School Bookstore, 1947.

They Went to Japan: Biographies of Missionaries of the Disciples of Christ. Indianapolis: Missionary Education Department, United Christian Missionary Society, 1948.

Trout, Jessie M. *Bertha Fidelia: Her Life*. Springport, Ind.: Springport Christian Church, 1992.

———. *Christianity in Japan*. Nashville: Disciples of Christ Historical Society, n.d.

West, Earl. *The Search for the Ancient Order*. Vol. 3. Delight, Ark.: Gospel Light Publishing Co., 1979.

———. *The Search for the Ancient Order*. Vol. 4. Delight, Ark.: Gospel Light Publishing Co., 1987.

PERIODICALS

Booster's Bulletin. Don Carlos Janes, ed. Louisville, Kentucky.

Minutes of the General Assembly of the Cumberland Presbyterian Church. 1902, 1904, 1905, 1936, 1957.

Missionary Messenger. J. M. McCaleb, C.G. Vincent, eds. Tokyo, Japan.

Tokyo Christian. W. D. Cunningham, ed. Tokyo, Japan.

Word and Work. R. H. Boll, ed. Louisville, Kentucky.

World Call. W. R. Warren, ed. (1919–1929); Bess White Cochran, ed. (1929–1932); Harold E. Fey, ed. (1932–1934); George W. Buckner, ed. (1935–1960).

ARTICLES

"Ada Calista Scott," *Christian Evangelist* 84 (October 30, 1946): 1086

Andrews, Sarah. "Sister Andrews Relates Japanese Experiences," *Gospel Advocate* 88 (November 14, 1946): 1076.

———. "My Maintenance During the War," *Gospel Advocate* 88 (November. 13, 1946): 919.

———. "Reports and Plans of Work in Japan," *Gospel Advocate* 88 (November. 20, 1947): 950.

Azbill, W. K. "Miss Miller's Mission," *Christian Evangelist* 31 (June 14, 1894): 610.

Berry, Minta Sue. "Sarah Andrews: Dickson's own Ambassador to Japan," *Dickson Herald*, 2001: A1.

Bradley, I. B. "Mission Appeal," *Gospel Advocate* 57 (July 22, 1915): 720.

———. "Funds for Sister Andrews," *Gospel Advocate* 57 (September 23, 1915): 955.

Brazelton, Howard J. "A Missionary Little Known," *Christian Standard* 49 (March 1, 1913): 28

"Broadway Mission in Japan," *Christian Standard* 47 (November 18, 1911): 7

"Crittenden Home Mission Work in Japan," *New York Times* 20 (June 29, 1913): 20

Cunningham, W. D. "Death of a Veteran Missionary," *Christian Standard* 64 (March 31, 1928): 8.

Doyle, Charles. "Sarah Andrews Succumbs to Stroke," *Firm Foundation* 78 (October 3, 1961): 637.

"Dr. Kelly," *The Missionary Record* 29 (August 1904): 189-190.

Ewing, George. "Hettie Lee Ewing," *Gospel Advocate* 131 (November 1989): 48-49.

Farnham, Grace. "Just Off the 'Gripsholm'," *Christian Standard* 79 (December 25, 1943): 1, 24.

Garst, Gretchen. "A Tribute to Miss Wirick," *Missionary Tidings* (October 1914): 215.

"Goes to Japan," *The Christian Builder* (August 15, 1935): 1, 3.

Indiana School Journal. 31 (July 1886): 397.

"Inez Helen Scott," *Christian Evangelist* 91 (January. 20, 1954): 6.

J. A. H. "Missionary on the Way to Japan," *Gospel Advocate* 46 (February 9, 1904): 8.

"Japanese Recognize Loduska Wirick, Native of Cedar County As 'Miss Nightingale of Orient,'" *The Tipton Conservative,* April 20, 1983. Social News Section.

Kelley, Carrie G. "Kuling, China," *The Missionary Record* 27 (January 1902): 20.

"Loduska J. Wirick, A Missionary to Japan," *The Studebaker Family* 5 (Fall 1984): 1-2.

Madden, Maude W. "Cecile Harding," *Christian Standard* 64 (February 9, 1929): 144.

———. "Death of Miss Miller," *Christian Standard* 63 (June 23, 1928): 607.

Marlin, J. T. "Sarah Andrews Prepares for Return," *Gospel Advocate* 90 (April 29, 1948): 419.

McCaleb, J. M. "Moving Pictures," *Gospel Advocate* 83 (November 27, 1941): 1147.

———. "Indirect News From Japan," *Gospel Advocate* 84 (April 9, 1942): 454.

———. "Another Worker for Japan," *Gospel Advocate* 57 (June 10, 1915): 574.

McCord, Hugo. "Sarah Andrews," *Firm Foundation* 114 (December 1999): 13-14.

McMillan, E. W. "A Noble Phoebe Has Passed," *Gospel Advocate* 103 (October 19, 1961): 662.

Miller, Alice. "Christmas Meeting at Sendagaya," *Christian Standard* 51 (February 12, 1916): 18.

Miller, Mary Rioch. "The Beginnings of Our Work in Japan," *The Canadian Disciple* (October 1930): 4-6.

"Missionary Dies," *Christian Evangelist* 94 (March 6, 1957): 310.

Nomura, Motoyuki. "Miss Nightingale of the Orient," *20th Century Christian* 47 (November 1984): 8-10.

Novak, Cindy. "Anxious For Nothing: Sarah Andrews," *20th Century Christian* 47 (November 1984): 29-31.

Pack, Frank. "Three Women in Missions," *20th Century Christian* 47 (November 1984): 24-25.

Robert, Dana L. "The Influence of American Missionary Women on the World Back Home," *Religion and American Culture: A Journal of Interpretation* 12 (2002): 59-89.

Shoemaker, Floyd C., ed. "Missourians in Japan," *Missouri Historical Review* 15 (October 1920–July 1921): 486.

"Sister of Local Man Was Held by Japanese," *Lakeland Ledger* (September 11, 1946): 14.

"The Death of Mrs. Kelly," *The Missionary Record* 27, (March 1902): 58, 60-61.

West, Earl. "War and Peace of Mind," *Gospel Advocate* 138 (February 1996): 36-37.

Wilson, Bert. "Miss Kate Johnson Called," *Christian Standard* 54 (February 15, 1919): 483

Wilson, Carolyn Taylor. "Women of the Restoration Movement—and Beyond." Paper presented to presidents of our Christian colleges, Nashville, November 15, 2005.

Young, Helen. "Sarah Andrews: She Dreamed a Dream for Japan," *21st Century Christian* 56 (November 1993): 7-9.

Young, Thomas A. "Death of Miss Loduska J. Wirick," *Christian Standard* 50 (June 13, 1914): 1062.

INTERNET SOURCES

"330th June Missions of 1945." www.rootsweb.com/~ny330bg/missionsjune.htm (accessed January 1, 2007).

Burger, Wayne, "Meditating on the Word: Sarah Andrews," IX, 18 (May 2, 2004). www.columbinechurchofchrist.org/printmeditating.php?id=642 (accessed October 9, 2007).

"Fire in the Night," *Time* (July 2, 1945). http://www.time.com/time/magazine/article/0,9171,775987,00.html (accessed August 12, 2007).

"Grace Braley, State Dept Interpreter, Dies," *The Washington Post* (March 9, 1990). http://www.highbeam.com/doc/lP2-1114680.html (accessed January 5, 2008).

"Japan Missions 1883-1983." http://www.bible101.org/japanmissions.htm (accessed February 4, 2008).

OTHER SOURCES

Personal Correspondence:

Andrews, Sarah. Letters to family, October 29, 1945; November 20, 1945.

———. Letters to J. M. McCaleb, September 6, 1946-August 5, 1950.

———. Letters to Harry Robert Fox Jr., January 7, 1952-June 5, 1956.

Ewing, Hettie Lee. Letter to J. M. McCaleb, August 23, 1946.

Farnham, Grace. Letter to unnamed friends, October 6, 1947.

Fox, Harry Robert Jr. Letters to Bettie Lundy, June 6, 2005-September 19, 2005.

Kashiwagi, Iki Naemura. Letters to Karene Harris, August 13, 1981; June 22, 1985.

Sutherland, Lois Smyser. Letter to Motoyuki Nomura, September 15, 1982.

INDEX

The Story of Churches of Christ

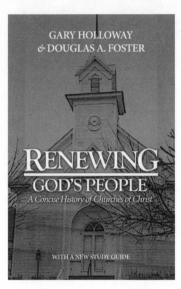

GARY HOLLOWAY
& DOUGLAS A. FOSTER

RENEWING
GOD'S PEOPLE
A Concise History of Churches of Christ

WITH A NEW STUDY GUIDE

*"**Renewing God's People** will become the standard text for passing down our history to the next generation."*

—Thomas H. Olbricht, author of *Hearing God's Voice*

With a new Study Guide

"There has rarely been a time when Churches of Christ have so needed to read and study a book like this one by Foster and Holloway. It is a fresh and fair treatment of the American heritage of Churches of Christ and their distinctive plea for New Testament Christianity. It is well designed for either serious study and discussion by classes or for casual, personal reading. Everyone would do well to read and think about this important book."

—Lynn McMillon, Dean, College of Biblical Studies, Oklahoma Christian University

176 pages $14.99
ISBN 0-89112-010-6

ACU
P R E S S
Abilene, Texas

To order call toll free **1-877-816-4455**
Or visit our website: **www.acupressbooks.com**
Or ask for it at your favorite bookstore